365
Powerful, Positive
Thoughts to Start Your Day

I AM POSITIVE!

by Mike Jones

365
Powerful, Positive
Thoughts to Start Your Day
I AM POSITIVE!

Cover design by Karol Hartzell
Interior design by Karol Hartzell

Printed in the United States of America.

ISBN-13 978-0-9833305-1-6
ISBN-10 0-9833305-1-6

First Edition
1 2 3 4 5 6 7 8 9 10

Mike Jones
Discover Leadership Training
3878 Robichaux Rd
Brookshire, TX 77423
713-807-9902
www.discoverleadership.com
info@discoverleadership.com

DEDICATION

This book, of powerful, positive thoughts, is dedicated to my four boys. My commitment is to help my four sons see they will become what they think about every day. It is my commitment to show them positive and negative exist in everything, and they are ALWAYS at choice as to which they are the most committed to choosing. I continue to focus on each of them becoming more positive, every day.

This book is my gift to them, and to you.
Choose positive.

INTRODUCTION

I have often said to people that there are 86,400 seconds in everyday and I believe it is possible to be positive in every one of them. I believe that we as human beings have a right to believe whatever we choose to believe. It is not necessary for me to make you wrong in order for me to be right. I will continue to believe what I believe until someone can show me something different and because I know I occupy the largest room in the house and that is the room for improvement, I remain open to learning new things and becoming aware of what I am unaware of in this present moment. If you do not agree with that, this book is not focused on making you wrong; I believe that would be negative.

If you will take a moment to just open your mind to a new possibility, I will share with you why I believe it is possible to be positive every second of everyday.

I believe as human beings, no matter what our conditions are we possess the gift of choice. Now I understand that there will be a tremendous amount of circumstances that will occur that we have NO control over, however, it is important to realize that the reality you are about to experience will be the result of the choice you make.

I submit that there is positive and negative in everything. One of them cannot exist without the other. Positive and negative are always a comparison to each other and what is so cool about that awareness is, I must know the other exist for me to make an assessment of either of them, now that is some Smokin' Hottt Shit!

When a circumstance occurs, it is "what is" until you make an assessment of it. The assessment that you make will be the result of your expectations or the socially agreed on expectations of how it was supposed to turn out. If it turned out the way you expected it would, then you assess it as positive. If it did not turn out the way you expected it to, you will assess it as negative. The best way to shift this way of thinking is to understand there is a universal conspiracy going on and that conspiracy is focused on your success. As soon as you understand and accept that truth, your life will be transformed forever.

It will be important for you to see how you are creating your reality. As soon as you assess the circumstance, "what is" as negative you have created a predictable negative future. And because every thought produces an action that is a likeness of itself, positive thoughts will produce positive actions and negative thoughts will produce negative actions. You must understand, this is not happening to you, it is happening because of you and your choices, so check the conversation you are having with yourself.

This book is focused on having you begin every day with a positive foundation and, in order to create an opportunity for optimal success, I have some coaching for you.

FIRST:

Move your alarm clock across the room. Make a commitment to yourself that when the alarm goes off, you will get up and remain up. I submit that every time you hit the snooze button, you are engaged in a negative conversation with yourself. Never hit the snooze button again. Never again deliberately choose to divert living for another second.

SECOND:

Read a positive thought from this book. Deliberately start visualizing ways, personally and professionally, that apply the message today.

THIRD:

The way to become more positive is to repeatedly practice being more positive. Practicing mental reps is to create the positive action in your mind before you do it. An example might be to smile and say, "Good Morning!" to the first person you encounter once you leave your residence. Find a way throughout your day to "catch people doing things right" and tell them what they did right.

FOURTH:

Deliberately make sure that you are focused on what you want and not what you don't want. Example: Most people feel that to focus on losing weight or getting out of debt is positive. I submit that is focused on what you don't want and that it is negative. Remember, every thought produces a likeness of itself. I submit that if you are focused on the positive that you want, your focus should be on getting healthier or financial security. If weight is a part of it, identify the target weight you are focused on achieving. If it is money, set a "by when" that you will pay off your bills and a "how much" you will save each month.

Be aware that words create pictures. Look at the different pictures created between losing 30 pounds and getting healthier. One is running from pain, the other is running to gain. It is absolutely possible to be positive all of the time, so I encourage you to make the choice to do so. Practice these techniques daily and positive will become your new normal and you will produce more of what you want every day.

JANUARY 1

You may recognize how easy it is to travel the path of least resistance; however, you will never create anything special or memorable by doing so. Today, challenge yourself to grow by not accepting the easy way and understanding that the reward usually mirrors the risk. You do not have 364 more days to do this; you only have today.

HAPPY NEW YEAR!

I AM POSITIVE!

JANUARY 2

It is important to know
that the biggest energy in an environment will prevail.
If you find yourself in a negative environment you must
be more positive than the negative energy in order to
overcome it. Let's be clear about this, your attitude
is not controlled by what is happening to you,
however it is controlled by the conversation you
are having with yourself. Remain focused on being
positive. We will make this the best first week
of the year ever.

I AM POSITIVE!

JANUARY 3

Create the life you want, do not wait. Do not wait for someone else to change their life in order for you to have the life you want.

I AM POSITIVE!

JANUARY 4

The only thing that you OWN in the universe is your word. Treat it as the valuable asset that it is and only give it when you are committed to producing a positive return by keeping your commitment.

I AM POSITIVE!

JANUARY 5

There are NO victims, only volunteers. You have
100% control of you and nothing else.

I AM POSITIVE!

JANUARY 6

Today is the best day in your life to take
100% personal responsibility for everything that is
going on in your life. Okay, now do it again tomorrow.

I AM POSITIVE!

JANUARY 7

If you've been waiting to bring your dreams to life,
then I have great news for you. Today is the day you've
been waiting for! This is the day when you can
truly begin to make your dreams reality.

I AM POSITIVE!

JANUARY 8

Commit today to let go of the excuses, no matter how reasonable they might sound. Remind yourself that there's something positive and meaningful you can do right now to make your dreams a reality. Then get yourself busy doing it.

I AM POSITIVE!

JANUARY 9

When life presents you with a challenge, take it.
Then celebrate the opportunity to authenticate
your commitment, passion, and enthusiasm to
live life full out.

I AM POSITIVE!

JANUARY 10

A person is not finished when they are defeated.
They are finished when they quit. As you work toward
your outcome there may come moments where you
encounter barriers or circumstances; embrace them.
The barriers and circumstances are gifts. This is your
opportunity to change your approach - pick yourself up,
dust yourself off, and keep moving forward.
Success will not be found in checking out and
accepting defeat; however, it could be just around
that next corner... so move your butt.

I AM POSITIVE!

JANUARY 11

Have the courage to create an image of the life you want.
Visualize it, write a story about it, and continually create
a conversation focused on making it a reality.
By doing these things, you will help identify the
behaviors that will keep you moving forward.
You really are worth it.

I AM POSITIVE!

JANUARY 12

There is no finish line. I have heard many people say that when they get the right job then they will be happy. The right job doesn't bring happiness. Well, when I get married, have children, send my children to college, retire, etc.; none of those events will make you happy. Happiness is something you decide ahead of time. Life is a journey, not a destination. "Not Over"

I AM POSITIVE!

JANUARY 13

Many of us who began the journey of personal growth and self-awareness have gained insight and knowledge about ourselves that we did not have prior to having started that courageous journey. You may have some people in your life who are not willing to take those same steps. Remember, it is impossible to awaken a person who is pretending to be asleep. Have the courage to continue moving forward with armor on the front, no holding back!

I AM POSITIVE!

JANUARY 14

True conviction about your values is having the courage to be authentically who you choose to be no matter who you are with.

I AM POSITIVE!

JANUARY 15

Discover Leadership Training talks a lot about
taking a 14 inch journey from your head to your heart.
Anyone who has embarked upon this very tough journey
would agree that this is likely the toughest journey
anyone will ever take. When you have the courage to
do so, you will find that seeing is not believing,
seeing is seeing. Our eyes provide sight; however,
our hearts provide insight.

I AM POSITIVE!

JANUARY 16

I have observed that there are a larger number of
people that are grinning and bearing the pain
of compromise, than those courageous enough to
take up arms against the opposition that wants to
keep them in the land of pretending.
Have the courage today to fight "for" what you want.

I AM POSITIVE!

JANUARY 17

Every one of us is an artist. Your thinking creates a
sculpture signifying how you lived your life. Take a step
back today and look at what you have created
so far and determine if you are creating the masterpiece
you want to leave with those you care most about.

I AM POSITIVE!

JANUARY 18

If you choose to focus on your potential of succeeding,
you will have more success than if you focus on your
potential of failure. I'm just sayin'.

I AM POSITIVE!

JANUARY 19

Every ceiling, when reached, becomes the foundation to get to your next level. Celebrate the climb and continue to climb. Regardless of your age, the color of your skin or your position in life, for every individual drawing breath in this world, there is one reality. It's Not Over until you say it's over...and by the way, old dogs learn new tricks every day.

I AM POSITIVE!

JANUARY 20

If your mind is focused on doubt and fear, you will not focus on the journey to what you want. The scars of our past indicate where we have been. Those scars do not have to determine where we are going.

I AM POSITIVE!

JANUARY 21

In order to be more successful you must see the
world simultaneously as it is and as it can become.
Now, all that you need to do is understand what needs
to happen to fill the gap between the two. Make a
commitment to TAN (Take Action Now),
and do those things now.

I AM POSITIVE!

JANUARY 22

If thoughts of doubt, fear, worry, doom and gloom, and focusing on what could go wrong are a part of your thoughts today, be responsible for eradicating those thoughts. They will never benefit you.

I AM POSITIVE!

JANUARY 23

One of the greatest enemies to potential is success.
Refuse to be satisfied with yesterday's success.
Today presents brand new possibilities for you to
redefine your 100%. If you are still celebrating yesterday's
successes, it is very likely you are not accomplishing
anything today. Focus today on besting your best.
Allow your best to be your evaluation of how well you
are doing. Keep on growing my friend.

I AM POSITIVE!

JANUARY 24

What you fight against weakens you. You have a choice to be independent of the opinions of others. Accept the fact that they are entitled to their opinion, just as you are entitled to yours. The energy you waste making them wrong will never benefit you in a positive way. The only benefit you will receive is you will get to be "right".

I AM POSITIVE!

JANUARY 25

If you have the courage to go for the things that bring you joy and make you happy, the people closest to you will tell you how much they support you. What you may become aware of is that they mean, "I support you if you do this the way I want you to do it." If you choose to move forward, it might get a little lonely; however, I promise you will never be alone.

I AM POSITIVE!

JANUARY 26

At Discover Leadership Training we believe that "I am" are two of the most powerful words you will ever speak because those two words identify the stories you tell yourself and others about you. Those two words indicate what you own as "truth". So, who are you?

1. I am _____

2. I am _____

3. I am _____

4. I am _____

5. I am _____

6. I am _____

7. I am _____

(Make a list of your top 7 positive "I Am' that you will choose to be.)

I AM POSITIVE!

JANUARY 27

No matter what you have accomplished in your life, success is never final unless you become complacent. No matter how hard you have fallen while going for what you want, failure is never fatal or the end unless you decide not to get up. As you choose to create success around you, it is important to see that success as the stair step to your next level. To remain committed to moving forward and redefining your 100%, to push yourself from what has become comfortable into the unknown, that my friend, will take courage. You've got this.

I AM POSITIVE!

JANUARY 28

It is not necessary to make them wrong in order
for you to be right. Are you tracking?

I AM POSITIVE!

JANUARY 29

We spend a tremendous amount of time and money looking for answers to what went wrong and whose fault it is. When we focus on what went wrong, the only benefit is that we now know who to blame.

I AM POSITIVE!

JANUARY 30

Psssssst... I have a little secret I want to share with you today. In order to get what you want from life, you must know what you want and then believe you can have it. Life is Great!

I AM POSITIVE!

JANUARY 31

Allow your passion, enthusiasm and conviction for the things you believe in to exude from you with the awareness that they will live beyond you. What will those closest to you say about you when you are gone?

I AM POSITIVE!

FEBRUARY

FEBRUARY 1

The moment you totally commit yourself and begin giving
100 percent to what you say you want, a certain momentum de-
velops. Total commitment and accepting personal
responsibility results in a certain magical boldness -
a boldness that has genius and power that are evident
based on the fruit produced by your actions.
How sweet is your fruit?

I AM POSITIVE!

FEBRUARY 2

When you believe you are ready, in that moment you are ready. Being optimistic means you have the faith to believe that what you want is possible. I have good news for you today. You are right.

I AM POSITIVE!

FEBRUARY 3

It has been said that the sweetest fruit available is out on the skinny branches; it requires you to risk something to go for it. It is okay to play full out today. Take the leap onto the skinny branch to get the fruit you want. If you want a significant reward, you must take a significant risk. Go for it now. Life is not a Dress Rehearsal.

I AM POSITIVE!

FEBRUARY 4

The only impossibilities that exist along life's journey
are within the conversation that you are having with yourself.
That conversation reveals what you are focused on and
determines the results you will ultimately produce. If you
are focused on your fears, what could go wrong, or doubting
your own ability to create success, then you will become
a prophet. Check the conversation that you are having
with yourself and focus on your outcome because
what you focus on will expand.

I AM POSITIVE!

FEBRUARY 5

During a recent flight I observed a woman with several magazines that chronicled what was going on in the personal lives and relationships of others. I wondered as I observed her, "How is it that we spend more time keeping up with and scrutinizing what is going on in others' lives than we do our own?" Why not make that investment in your personal growth and your relationships?

I AM POSITIVE!

FEBRUARY 6

Emotions can ignite action; however, emotions rarely
sustain the action taken. You must focus on a positive
outcome and remain focused on that positive outcome
in order to sustain it. TAN (Take Action Now) and write down the
benefits of your outcome. Allow those benefits to fuel
your next step. Now, didn't that feel better?

I AM POSITIVE!

FEBRUARY 7

One of my gifts is that when I look at people, I see their potential. What I have been made aware of time and time again is that potential does not equate to character. I have learned that when all is said and done, it will not matter at the end of the game what the score is. What will matter is how you played the game.

I AM POSITIVE!

FEBRUARY 8

Today I am going to let you in on a little secret... Shhhh. Control is an illusion. If you focus on controlling a particular situation or person, you will never enjoy the beauty of simply "being" with them. So, instead of seeking control, start being in the moment and enjoy each moment.

I AM POSITIVE!

FEBRUARY 9

Unless you do something beyond what you have already mastered, you will never grow to your next level of personal development. We all occupy the largest room in the house - the room for improvement. If you have become comfortable with the place you are, and you remain there, you are dying and decaying. When you get out of your comfort zone, push yourself, challenge yourself, and stretch beyond your present successes, you will be green and growing. There is always another level to be reached; after all, it's NOT OVER!

I AM POSITIVE!

FEBRUARY 10

Accepting personal responsibility may mean facing
the music, even when you do not like the tune. I encourage
you to remain focused on your positive outcome today
in the midst of the storm you are going through.
That circumstance may be tough; however, it will be
rewarding to identify the benefits of focusing on the
positive and taking the next step. You are one step
away from a brighter day.

I AM POSITIVE!

FEBRUARY 11

The only limitations to your ability to do whatever it takes today to get one step closer to your outcome will be your failures and doubts from yesterday. The conversation you are having with yourself will create the energy and actions you will deliver in this present moment and that will produce the reality you are experiencing. Generally, limitations only identify your capacity to believe that what you want is possible. You must believe it, before you see it.

I AM POSITIVE!

FEBRUARY 12

Every circumstance in your life will make you bitter or better. Every circumstance you experience has the potential of making you or breaking you. The choice is yours to become a victim or become victorious. The choice that you make will be to the thing you are the MOST committed to. Both are available right now. Choose one.

I AM POSITIVE!

FEBRUARY 13

Whether you are having a great day or a bad day will not be determined by what is happening in your world today. A great day or a bad day is determined by your assessment of what is happening – you are a prophet... so, why not prophesize a great day? I'm just sayin'.

I AM POSITIVE!

FEBRUARY 14

The person who is willing to best their best and
go beyond excellence is reinventing them self.
Who you "BE" speaks so loud, that others can't even
hear what you are saying. Determine those values that
are significant to you – honesty, confidence, passion,
trust – and make the choice to "BE" that in such a way
that every action you take, every step on your journey,
is redefined because of you. So who are you????
That is exactly who they will become.

I AM POSITIVE!

FEBRUARY 15

Every day you are on this earth, you have two options
with how to live that day. You can either make the choice
to get in the game, have the courage to get out on those
skinny branches to reap the sweetest fruit or you can
sit on the sidelines, stuck within your comfort zone,
waiting to die. Living a life on purpose requires you to
identify an outcome or purpose that you are focused on.
Then, you must have the courage to play full out.
The adventure is before you and the choice is
ultimately yours. You are worthy of that sweet fruit.

I AM POSITIVE!

FEBRUARY 16

No matter what circumstances or pain you have
experienced in your life, you were not born by accident.
The miracle and purpose of your existence is in your hands.
It will be okay to get this handled before you leave.
I'm just sayin'.

I AM POSITIVE!

FEBRUARY 17

If you are experiencing any frustration in any of your relationships today, my coaching to you is to write down what is creating the frustration. Now that you can see it, my coaching to you is to never allow that to happen again. Frustration is produced when you internalize a conversation about an unfulfilled expectation. When you communicate what you just wrote down to that person, you at least create a possibility that you will never be frustrated again. That coaching is worth a million dollars if you execute it. No need to write a check, this one is on the house.

I AM POSITIVE!

FEBRUARY 18

We have been taught that choosing yourself first is selfish. Unselfishness is not available to you until you choose yourself first. You cannot give away what you do not have. Unselfishness is not a concept; it is a gift. If you need an example of this truth, consider the result of focusing on saving everyone on an airplane before saving yourself first if the cabin becomes depressurized.

I AM POSITIVE!

FEBRUARY 19

It is predictable that you will continue to experience frustration with your significant other if you continue managing your relationship based on expectations. Take the time to identify what the two of you are committed to, then make and manage the promises to deliver. When you do, "I love you" will take on a new meaning.

I AM POSITIVE!

FEBRUARY 20

In order to be an outstanding leader, you will need to appeal to the hearts of the members of your TEAM at work and at home, not their minds. The toughest journey we will ever make is just 14 inches; it is the trip from your head to your heart. Until you have the courage to make that journey, you will never inspire yourself or those around you to lead from the heart.

I AM POSITIVE!

FEBRUARY 21

I submit that the best way to see the world through someone else's eyes is with your ears. Listening to the story others are telling allows us to see what they see. Hearing is etiquette; however, listening is the most effective way to love people the way they want to be loved and to honor them the way they want to be honored. This awareness is my gift to you today. Life is Great!

I AM POSITIVE!

FEBRUARY 22

No matter the color of your skin or your cultural beliefs, there was a prescribed way of living your life in place before you were born. I submit that if you choose to follow the prescription, you will live a predictable life and it will be comfortable; however, a life on purpose, creating new possibilities, experiencing true happiness, knowing real joy, realizing authentic love, and making the impossible, possible may not never happen for you. There is no need to make someone else wrong in order for you to do what is right for you. Do it today.

I AM POSITIVE!

FEBRUARY 23

There is no reason, no excuse, no alibi, and no fate, that can hinder an individual that is focused on a specific purpose. You are in control of the direction you are moving. Nothing outside of you chooses your path. To understand this is to accept personal responsibility for where you are in this present moment, the choices you have made, and the results those choices have produced. Establish your direction, your outcome, and make the choice to TAN (Take Action Now). This sets you in motion and the commitment and resolve that you demonstrate will keep you focused on your purpose.

I AM POSITIVE!

FEBRUARY 24

Never settle for Good-Nuff.
It will never be enough.
Nuff said.

I AM POSITIVE!

FEBRUARY 25

It is a Great Day to be Alive! It does not matter what the weather is outside today, a bright sunny day is a way of "being". Be the sunny day in your life today and brighten someone else's day as well. Life is Great!

I AM POSITIVE!

FEBRUARY 26

Have you ever noticed how passionate people are about what they don't want? What would it be like if we demonstrated that same passion about what we do want? The thought of that just gave me a chill. Okay, what will you do today to test this out? What do you stand for?

I AM POSITIVE!

FEBRUARY 27

There are no finish lines in life. Even death is
not a destination; however, the way we live our lives
today will live on even after we are gone. What legacy
are you creating today? What will they say about you
when you are gone?

I AM POSITIVE!

FEBRUARY 28

When you accept 100% personal responsibility for
your thoughts, you will have 100% control over the
realities in your life. Now, that does not submit that
everything will turn out the way you wanted it to,
it means that you will have done 100% of what you knew
to do to get to that outcome. I believe that is success.

I AM POSITIVE!

FEBRUARY 29

LEAP YEAR

As long as you are living your life based on the expectations others have of you and living by their rules, you will never be happy, fulfilled or successful; well, unless your outcome is to simply live your life pleasing others.

I AM POSITIVE!

MARCH

MARCH 1

Many of the events you call failures occur because you did not realize how close you were to success in the moment you gave up. Quite often successes are found in the marathons of life, those that require perseverance and our commitment to see it through. Keep moving forward and realize that usually that last step is the toughest....but as tough as it is, it is the one that will ultimately get you to your success!

I AM POSITIVE!

MARCH 2

Thinking positively is not the end game.
I encourage you to keep moving forward and execute
on those positive thoughts in order to produce positive
actions, which in turn will produce a positive reality.

I AM POSITIVE!

MARCH 3

It is important to know where you are receiving your
personal daily currency. No matter where you have been
receiving your currency, it is important to be aware
that yesterday is a cancelled check, tomorrow is a
promissory note, and the only cash you have is today.
So, look within and be sure to pay yourself
today, because you are worth it.

I AM POSITIVE!

MARCH 4

When you understand there are many different
ways to look at everything, you will become aware that
every time you choose to look at the same thing
from different perspectives, you will see something
differently. How cool is that?

I AM POSITIVE!

MARCH 5

Are you living a life of significance or success?
Every time you step up to do something significant,
there will be negative naysayers. They are a gift;
you should embrace them. They will authenticate your
commitment to a life of creating a significant legacy.

I AM POSITIVE!

MARCH 6

True leaders have the confidence to stand alone, the courage to make tough decisions, and the compassion to listen to the needs of others. They do not set out to be a leader, yet become one by the quality of their actions and the integrity of their intent. In the end, leaders are much like eagles... They don't flock, you will find them one at a time... There is an "i" in team!

I AM POSITIVE!

MARCH 7

There is an "i" in Team, and the "I" is you!
You are either a creator of truth or a creature of
circumstance - you either bring color into your
environment or, like a chameleon, you take
color from others' environments. YOU MATTER!

I AM POSITIVE!

MARCH 8

I want you to be aware today that every journey begins with the first step. You will get closer to your outcome by continually taking steps and moving forward toward that outcome. What steps will you take today that will lead you to something that you really want in your life? I remind you that this is not a dress rehearsal. Today is the best day in your life to take that step.

I AM POSITIVE!

MARCH 9

Some people grin and bear it, while others smile
and TAN (Take Action Now) focused on creating a
positive outcome. There is a big difference in
running from pain and running to gain.
Set an outcome and focus on what you want.
"iFOTO" (I Focus On The Outcome) is my Motto.

I AM POSITIVE!

MARCH 10

You never know how far reaching something you think, say, or do today will affect the lives of the people on your professional and personal teams. YOU matter, YOU count. You affect everything that you touch either positively or negatively. PLEASE be aware there is NO neutral. Make the choice to create a positive environment through your positive attitude. Hmmmm...you never know how far that positive attitude will reach today.

I AM POSITIVE!

MARCH 11

If you really connect to this message today you
will become aware that you will never have to get
angry ever again. Anger is ALWAYS a secondary emotion.
Therefore, if you have the courage to address what
needs to be addressed in the moment, you will speed
up the transaction and then...no more anger.

I AM POSITIVE!

MARCH 12

It only takes one word to start a
conversation, one voice to speak with wisdom,
one hope to elevate a spirit, one step to begin a journey,
one laugh to conquer gloom, one candle to wipe out
darkness, one touch to show you care, and one person
to change the world. That person is you.

I AM POSITIVE!

MARCH 13

The mind is the decisive factor in your life's experience and I ask, "Who decides for the mind?" To think negatively is like taking a toxic drug; however, choosing to think positively produces strength, a positive attitude and initiative.

I AM POSITIVE!

MARCH 14

Failure is the refusal to give up all of that junk from your past that you do not need. The more you focus on that stuff, the more it controls the next choice that you make. Okay, this is not a conversation about getting over anything; it is, however, a conversation about getting on with it. So move your butt toward the positive stuff that you want.

I AM POSITIVE!

MARCH 15

If you spend all day deciding what to do with your
life, at the end of the day you will have done it.
I'm just sayin'.

I AM POSITIVE!

MARCH 16

If you continue "right fighting" with yourself and others to prove how weak you are, how ill-equipped you are, or how you can't do something, there is no need to wonder who will win that fight. That future has already been created. Congratulations! You got to be right. How's that working for you?

I AM POSITIVE!

MARCH 17

If you could project yourself to the end of your life and you could visualize a smile on your face and joy in your heart because you had a "Great Life", what would your story be? You will only experience that "Great Life" if you choose to create it. A "Great Life" will not happen to you; it will happen because of you.

I AM POSITIVE!

MARCH 18

People who are considered winners have lost or failed more than those who are considered losers. Winners lose more than losers because they accept personal responsibility to continue changing their approach until they get what they want. Unfortunately, losers who lose blame the weather, the economy, the color of their skin, their age, and many other things for not winning. What I am really saying here is some of the biggest losers I know are also some of the biggest winners I know. The only way to affect the score on the scoreboard is by getting into the game. You may lose every now and then which really means you won.

I AM POSITIVE!

MARCH 19

Everyone has value and something valuable to contribute.
DO NOT let "what you can't do" prevent you from
doing everything you can. Play FULL OUT and
give 100% of what you have to give!

I AM POSITIVE!

MARCH 20

Those dreams that you have had about the things you really, really want; it will be okay to wake up and make your dreams a reality, in fact that is the only way it will happen. Nuff said.

I AM POSITIVE!

MARCH 21

There is one answer to every question in the universe and that answer is YES! If you constantly tell yourself that you can't, you won't. If you constantly tell yourself you can, you will. WAYFO? (What Are You Focused On?) What you focus on will expand! Make a commitment to yourself to invent the positive future you want.
Life is Great!

I AM POSITIVE!

MARCH 22

Pain has gotten a bad rap and your comfort zone is far overrated. I often hear people say, "I don't need to change; I like me the way I am.". If you do not want to create any greater success as work and at home, then remain the way you are. If you want more out of your life, change will be necessary. I understand that it is sometimes painful; however the growth creates new possibilities. You are either green and growing or you are dying and decaying.

I AM POSITIVE!

MARCH 23

Being 100% honest with yourself will allow you to authenticate what is real for you. Most adults will not be true to themselves if they may look bad in the eyes of others. I encourage you to focus on becoming independent of the opinions of others and be true to yourself.

I AM POSITIVE!

MARCH 24

Can you imagine what it would be like to approach everything today with the enthusiasm of a child? Treating everything as if you are experiencing it for the first time. Well, if you can imagine it, it is possible to make it happen.

I AM POSITIVE!

MARCH 25

Measuring your wins and losses based upon someone else's successes and failures, will never be a true test of your potential. Comparing your 100% to another's is either limiting or self-defeating. Make the choice today to best your best in some area of your life. When you do, you will have redefined your 100%. Okay, that was really cool.
Let's do that again.

I AM POSITIVE!

MARCH 26

The best person to compare you to, is you.
Focus on getting to your next level and improving in
every aspect of your life. Guess what, someone out there
will not get this message and they are comparing themselves
to you. Give them something powerful and positive to
aspire to become. Find one way to best your
best in some area of your life today.

I AM POSITIVE!

MARCH 27

There is an "i" in team, IT'S YOU!! You matter, you count,
and you affect the outcome, positively or negatively,
in every professional and personal relationship.
Accept personal responsibility today to be positive no
matter the circumstance. Positive and negative are both
available to you in this present moment. Once you choose,
you identify what you are most committed to.
It's your choice.

I AM POSITIVE!

MARCH 28

In this present moment unreasonable possibilities exist. What do you have the capacity to believe? Most people immediately think about how they can get more money or be in a better relationship; however, those things are the fruit of accepting a higher calling to "BE" the CEO (Chief Example Officer) for what you say you believe. Life is Great!

I AM POSITIVE!

MARCH 29

Everything that has caused you pain in your life,
is behind you. Bringing your pain into your present
moment gives life to the pain to live another day.
The pain is not creating more pain, your choice is -
choose to move forward and live in the moment.
Blow-up every bridge that leads back to all
of it and move forward.

I AM POSITIVE!

MARCH 30

Leadership is not a mandate it is a choice...
so is following for that matter. Whether you are
following or leading do it because it is what is right for
you and your team in that moment. I submit the best
testament to a great leader is one who
produces more leaders, not more followers.
A true leader is not afraid to share their knowledge.

I AM POSITIVE!

MARCH 31

Everything that you fight against weakens you.
Failure is the refusal to give up what you don't need.
Holding on to things from past relationships that
hurt you means they continue to hurt you until
you choose to release them. Releasing those
negative things also releases you.

I AM POSITIVE!

APRIL

APRIL 1

Success consists of going from circumstance to circumstance without losing your focus or enthusiasm to realize your positive outcome. You will observe that the last 4 letters in the word "Enthusiasm" are IASM- which stands for "I Am Sold Myself!" Each circumstance you experience is a gift and represents a choice point, and it is in that moment that you get to authenticate your commitment to your outcome.
Wow, that is a powerful awareness.

I AM POSITIVE!

APRIL 2

Have you ever noticed how much anger and negativity
is required to fight against things you do not like or want?
Be aware that everything produces a likeness of itself.
If the seeds you plant are anger and negativity, that is
the fruit that will be produced. Tell me again how that
will benefit you or anyone else.

I AM POSITIVE!

APRIL 3

A positive attitude creates a chain reaction of positive thoughts. Every day you get to choose your attitude. Your quality of life will not be determined by the circumstances you experience today, rather 100% of your realities will be the result of how you react or respond to those circumstances. I'm just sayin'.

I AM POSITIVE!

APRIL 4

Focusing on the things that went wrong yesterday creates depression. Focusing on things that could go wrong tomorrow creates anxiety. One of the greatest gifts you have is choice, so choose to focus on this present moment! Give everything you have to making positive memories because whether positive or negative those memories will live on forever.
So, choose well my friend.

I AM POSITIVE!

APRIL 5

It is Indeed Another Great Day to be Alive! It really
does not matter what happened yesterday because you
do not have to be defined by your yesterdays.
Today you can begin again and the score is zero/zero -
an opportunity to create new opportunities - new possibilities
exist for you. You will create what you think about all day,
so WAYFO? (What Are You Focused On?)
It will be okay to think about how you will
positively approach this day.

I AM POSITIVE!

APRIL 6

When you are standing on the sidelines of life the things that you really, really want are not available to you. Unless you choose to get in the game and risk success, your only possession in the end will be woulda, coulda, shoulda. I'm just sayin'.

I AM POSITIVE!

APRIL 7

Teamwork is just work unless your team is focused on the same outcome. Once the outcome is clear to every member of your team, then a commitment is made to synergize all of the resources of the team to get to that outcome. Think of it this way... a team is much like an orchestra in which each member may be playing a different instrument; however, they are playing the same song in perfect harmony.

I AM POSITIVE!

APRIL 8

Everything you fight against weakens you. This is a message that
if just one person embraces today, the world will be a better place.
For every ounce of energy you spend fighting against the things
you don't want or do not like you will miss an opportunity to
positively affect what you do like and what you do want.
Are you expending your energy in such a way that it
is producing a positive return on your investment?
Because the choice you make right now will create
the future you are about to experience.

I AM POSITIVE!

APRIL 9

If you are experiencing anything you "don't want" in your life, it is because of what you are choosing. The choices you make in every moment are the things you are the most committed to.
You are 100% personally responsible for that choice. So what do you really want?

I AM POSITIVE!

APRIL 10

When you remain focused on a positive outcome,
when you remain personally responsible and committed
to achieve your positive outcome, there will be no mountain,
ocean, negative person, or circumstance that will prevent
you from achieving that positive outcome. Wow! I just started
the celebration of you making your positive outcome a reality.

I AM POSITIVE!

APRIL 11

One of my greatest discoveries for living a positive, focused, happy life is an awareness that everything in the universe is a gift. Even my enemies, because they give me an opportunity to authenticate what I say I believe, not by fighting against them, but instead fighting for what I believe by doing more of it.

I AM POSITIVE!

APRIL 12

There is a difference between doing the "right thing" and "doing things right". It is possible to do the wrong thing "right". So, how do you know when you are doing the "right thing"? When you set an outcome, focusing on that outcome allows you to determine the appropriateness of every choice you make.

I AM POSITIVE!

APRIL 13

Things no longer own you when you have the courage to detach from them. Everything you fight against weakens you and hinders your ability to see the positive opportunities in the obstacle. What are you holding on to that has passed its expiration date?

I AM POSITIVE!

APRIL 14

The best time to go for what you want is this "present moment". Time is a paradox, stretching between your past and your future and has no reality except in your mind. So, live in the moment. Go for what you want NOW with heart, body and soul.

I AM POSITIVE!

APRIL 15

Project yourself to what you want to become and
then begin acting as if you are already there.
When you do, you will activate the energy, behaviors,
and focus it will take to get there. If you are committed,
your dream is about to become reality.

I AM POSITIVE!

APRIL 16

Did you know that there are over 80 muscles in
your face? It's time to develop a morning workout plan.
Let's do this together... up... down... up... down...
That's it, you've got it. Now, go around the house and
office and keep working those muscles. Be the role model
and you will see others start doing the same exercises.

I AM POSITIVE!

APRIL 17

Every time I become aware of how a person sees themselves, my first question is, "What are you comparing yourself to?" Most people would argue they do not compare themselves to anything, and I submit that this is not the truth. If you see yourself as beautiful or ugly, you are comparing. If you see yourself as worthy or unworthy, you are comparing. Who are you comparing yourself to and why?

I AM POSITIVE!

APRIL 18

Taking action in the moment is leadership - not position or authority. The person who holds a higher position or who has authority is not automatically the leader. Leaders have the courage to TAN (Take Action Now) with no attachment to the outcome. It is in that choice to TAN that results are created and the vision becomes reality. Yes you guessed it, time to move your butt.

I AM POSITIVE!

APRIL 19

I was speaking to a stay at home mom after her husband had nominated her to attend our class. She said to me that she was not a leader and did not need to attend our program. I asked her if self-confidence, drive, passion, enthusiasm, self-worth and being positive were attributes of leadership and she agreed. I then asked her how would her children see the value in these leadership qualities if she did not demonstrate them? I informed her that everyone of us is the CEO (Chief Example Officer) of our lives because "who you BE, they will Become".

I AM POSITIVE!

APRIL 20

I have observed in my work that there is a large segment of the population that feels life is happening to them. Many feel they have no control of their feelings or reality. Check your Belief System because that is not the truth. The conversation you are having with yourself is determining your feelings, and the choices you are making are creating your reality.

I AM POSITIVE!

APRIL 21

The one common quality that I have observed in most successful leaders is the choice to accept personal responsibility for their outcomes. Choosing to accept personal responsibility means taking ownership for your choices and the consequences that each of those choices create. ANYTIME you blame something or someone else you give up the power to affect a positive outcome.

I AM POSITIVE!

APRIL 22

It is better to be respected than liked.
Effective leaders understand that there are times
when tough decisions will need to be made and
they choose to make them while remaining focused
on a positive outcome. Life is Great!

I AM POSITIVE!

APRIL 23

I want to let you in on something that is TOP SECRET...
there is a conspiracy going on that is focused on
your success. You have likely heard it said that
everything happens for a reason. Guess what?
It's true. Now it is up to YOU to find the positive in
what happened and celebrate. TAN (Take Action Now)!

I AM POSITIVE!

APRIL 24

When I speak to people about going for what they say they want, I am often told they are waiting for the "right time". If you choose to set a positive outcome, make a commitment to yourself to make it happen, surround yourself with the kind of people who will hold you accountable and support you and give your heart, body and soul to achieve the outcome, unexpectedly the "right time" becomes NOW! So, what again are you waiting for????

I AM POSITIVE!

APRIL 25

Children receive over 460 negative messages on average every day. So whether you are a parent or not I am requesting that you find a way to catch a young person doing something right today. Do something today that has the potential of creating a smile on their face. There are over 80 muscles in our face and it seems the older we get the less we exercise them.

I AM POSITIVE!

APRIL 26

Here is an awareness you may not have wanted to hear today. Every time you hit that snooze button on your alarm clock, think about the conversation you are having with yourself. Is that conversation positive or negative? Thanks for your honesty; it is negative. Knowing that positive and negative are choices, why would you ever choose negative? It's time to change your approach as to how you start your day.

I AM POSITIVE!

APRIL 27

When your eyes are focused on a specific positive outcome, obstacles are rarely seen. Once you have determined your positive outcome, the next step is to focus three feet and beyond that outcome. As long as you remain laser focused on where you are going, the choices necessary to get you there will be obvious, and the obstacles along the way will become mere stepping stones.
Remember – what gets your attention, gets YOU.

I AM POSITIVE!

APRIL 28

The famous actress, Lucille Ball once said, "I would rather regret the things that I have done than the things that I have not." I made a decision several years ago that caused me a tremendous amount of disappointment and pain. The results of that decision taught me so much about myself. If you become wiser from whatever you are doing why would you ever feel regret? Okay, let's stop the presses for one moment. If you are still blaming the person or the circumstance that caused you disappointment or pain then you will continue to have regrets, accepting personal responsibility for your choice regarding this situation will free you from regret. Okay, that is going to sting for a little while.

I AM POSITIVE!

APRIL 29

The time to go for what you want is NOW! There is nothing
that needs to be fixed and you are not lacking anything.
What stands between you and what you really want
is a choice. Take the first step NOW!

I AM POSITIVE!

APRIL 30

If you continue approaching things the same way you always have, it may be comfortable; however, the future is predictable. Change your approach and surprise yourself. Every time you change your approach, you create an opportunity for an "unreasonable possibility" to emerge. When was the last time you surprised yourself?

I AM POSITIVE!

MAY 1

You may be given the authority to lead, however,
without the respect, trust, and belief from those
who are meant to follow; you are just a figure head.
Authority is not leadership.

I AM POSITIVE!

MAY 2

When was the last time you focused on building a
healthy relationship with yourself? When was the last time you
made a promise to yourself to love you more, respect you more,
to be more self-confident, to smile more and be more positive?
When was the last time you caught yourself doing something
right? The healthier the relationship you have with yourself will
determine how healthy it is with others.

I AM POSITIVE!

MAY 3

Anytime you come to what appears to be the end
of anything, my coaching to you is to remain positive
and keep moving forward, it truly is not the end,
it is a new beginning.

I AM POSITIVE!

MAY 4

Be aware that if you are experiencing apprehension
and nervousness about an upcoming decision or
circumstance, that apprehension and nervousness is
being created by the conversation you are
having about the decision or circumstance.
Okay, so this takes a little practice, however, you can
start right now. Create a story about how much
benefit you will receive from taking this on and
replace the story you are telling yourself about
how scary it is... let me know how it goes.

I AM POSITIVE!

MAY 5

It is important to surround yourself with the kind of
people who will support you and hold you accountable
to play at a higher level and remain focused on your outcome.
Why would you set a positive outcome to become
an eagle and then surround yourself with chickens?
Let's rethink that approach because the predictable
future is you becoming a chicken.

I AM POSITIVE!

MAY 6

Today you can begin again. Whatever happened yesterday, happened. You do not have to be defined by your yesterdays, because the choice you are making right now is creating your reality in this present moment. Choose well my friend, by focusing on a positive outcome.

I AM POSITIVE!

MAY 7

A good leader inspires others to believe in them.
A great leader inspires others to believe in themselves.
We here at Discover Leadership Training submit that
there is an "I" in team, because each of us affects the
teams outcome positively or negatively.
Inspiring others to accept personal responsibility
will encourage them to own their place on the team.

I AM POSITIVE!

MAY 8

Love is a powerful force that can mend your heart or break it into a million pieces. Choose to give love that will mend hearts and choose to receive love that will mold the broken pieces back together again. Choose your words with care!

I AM POSITIVE!

MAY 9

We all occupy the largest room in the house -
the room for improvement. As long as you are living
on this earth, there is an opportunity for growth.
Keep moving forward, armor on the front, and
know that as you climb your current challenge...
heave yourself over the edge, take that deep breath
and look up... you will see there is another level
there waiting for you. Celebrate your accomplishment
of reaching your next level and celebrate that you
get to go the next level! It's "Not Over".

I AM POSITIVE!

MAY 10

You will truly begin living at peace and experience incredible joy in your life when you become independent of the opinions of others.

I AM POSITIVE!

MAY 11

As long as you continue to focus on the things that caused you pain, then you simply get to continue to have a good reason to justify your misery. My question to you today is, "How's that working for you?" Give yourself permission to get on with living your life; in fact, you are the only person that can give you permission to do so.

I AM POSITIVE!

MAY 12

Every time you assess something as being negative, you can be assured that there is a positive side of the exact same thing. In order to assess something as negative or positive it is a comparison to something. Once that comparison has been made, then a choice is determined. I believe that one of the greatest gifts that you have is the gift of choice. With that understanding, why would you ever choose to be negative?

I AM POSITIVE!

MAY 13

What comes out of you when the pressure is on is "who you BE". Situations and circumstances do not define you, they simply reveal the conversation that you are having with yourself. It is in those adverse circumstances or situations that your true character is revealed, and your conversation becomes amplified. In those moments – what is being revealed about you? Okay, good thing we got that worked out, because "who you BE, they will BEcome". I sure hope that is good news.

I AM POSITIVE!

MAY 14

You can choose to believe anything in the universe that you want... so why not choose to believe in yourself? Every situation that you face in life will reveal the authentic conversation you are in and will reveal your true belief in yourself in that moment. You become either your greatest advocate or your greatest challenge. You have the choice in each of those moments to believe in yourself and trust the potential that you have. Believing in yourself opens the door for that potential to be realized and creates possibilities that would not have existed otherwise. You matter, you count...

I AM POSITIVE!

MAY 15

Some people say, "The journey begins with the first step."
Well, I believe the journey begins with the first thought.
Until you think it and believe it, it won't happen, because
energy and action follow thought. Take a look at what
you are thinking. WAYFO? (What Are You Focused On?)

I AM POSITIVE!

MAY 16

In the context of this conversation, there are no victims,
only volunteers. If you are presently experiencing anything in
your life that you do not want, look within yourself for the answers.
Ask yourself, "What else can I do to create what I want?" and
then take personal responsibility for making it happen.
If you are willing to take personal responsibility, there is
no one else to blame. When the "observer" becomes the
"observed", new possibilities will emerge.

I AM POSITIVE!

MAY 17

Today is the best day in your life to get in the game
and play full out. Nothing will be accomplished if every
objection must be overcome before you TAN (Take Action Now)!

I AM POSITIVE!

MAY 18

There is a significant price to be paid if you expect to achieve GREATNESS in your professional and personal lives, the price is accepting Personal Responsibility for everything going on in your life.

I AM POSITIVE!

MAY 19

When you say you "can't" do something it will
create a predictable future and you won't.
When you say you "can" you have just communicated
that there is potential in your future. When you say
you "will" and you are committed, you will have
created a future "I did".

I AM POSITIVE!

MAY 20

When faced with a tough circumstance, take a moment to decide what positive outcome you are committed to, then go for it heart, body, and soul. Spending any time worrying about what could go wrong will never benefit you. Focus on what you want and accept personal responsibility to make it happen.

I AM POSITIVE!

MAY 21

Who will you choose to be today to improve
your relationships at work and home? I suspect
you may still be waiting for them to do something
different to improve the relationship. Well, how is
that working for you? Have the courage to
be a "Game Changer", take the first step.

I AM POSITIVE!

MAY 22

In order to have the absolute, most positive day
of your life today, I recommend that you set it as
your outcome today and accept personal responsibility
to make it happen. If you are waiting for anyone else
to create it for you, it may never happen.
This is your NOW, and this IS the best day in your
life to begin living on purpose. What will you do
today to be more positive?

I AM POSITIVE!

MAY 23

It's the morning again and yes, every day starts with a morning. Treat this morning as if it is the only one you have. Oh my, it is the only morning you have in this present moment. Choose to play full out this morning; you will never see this one again. Life is Great!

I AM POSITIVE!

MAY 24

If you have never failed at anything, it is predictable that you are playing small. Failure or falling down has been given a bad rap. When you get out of your comfort zone and go for the things you REALLY, REALLY want, you risk success, not failure. Learning from failure is an incredible gift and brings you one step closer to your success. So get out there and play full out today.

I AM POSITIVE!

MAY 25

Life is Great! Nuff said.

I AM POSITIVE!

MAY 26

During our training we address the #1 fear of mankind...
public speaking. Did you know that the #2 fear of
mankind is death by fire? Now, let me put this
into perspective, most people would rather be
the charred remains in the casket than the
person standing up to give the eulogy.
Think about that and send me an email
if you want to get that #1 fear handled.

I AM POSITIVE!

MAY 27

I understand that "iFOTO" (I Focus On The Outcome)
is a simple concept, however, it is not simple to perform.
It is important to become aware that whatever you
choose to focus on will expand. So, practice remaining
focused on your positive outcome; the outcome will
determine the next step you will need to take to get
closer to that outcome. iFOTO is my Motto.

I AM POSITIVE!

MAY 28

Every one of us occupies the largest room in the house, that's the room for improvement. Everyone you meet knows something that you do not. Choose to redefine your personal 100% daily by being willing to learn from others and best your best. The focus does not need to be on fixing what's wrong; the focus can be on getting to the next level.

I AM POSITIVE!

MAY 29

I am going out on a limb, Oh WOW, what a great idea.
Isn't it out on a limb that you will find the sweetest fruit?
I am going to offer a disclaimer: If you choose to step
out on a limb you could fall. However, if you do not
take that step you will never taste the sweetest fruit
on the tree. It is time to make a choice because
there is a crowd waiting for the fruit to fall.

I AM POSITIVE!

MAY 30

The attitude that you are choosing in this present moment is contagious. Everyone around you is being infected with your attitude. Your team is either focused on embracing your positive attitude or they are focused on overcoming your negative attitude. There is an "i" in team. Yep, you guessed correctly, it's you.

I AM POSITIVE!

MAY 31

You will not be defined by the stuff that you have
or the stuff you wanted and never acquired.
It's really cool to set outcomes to acquire stuff
and make it happen, however, the stuff is not you.
You will not be remembered for what you got, you
will be remembered for what you gave.
Givers Gain. Life is Great!

I AM POSITIVE!

JUNE 1

Shakespeare said, "To thine own self be true."
When you choose to be honest with yourself about
where you are and how you feel about things, it will speed
up your opportunity to get to your next level. Tell yourself
the truth today, about how you can improve one of your
relationships and accept 100% personal responsibility
to best your best in that relationship.
Wow, did you feel that? It was a shift in the
universe and it happened because of you.
Pick another relationship and do that again.

I AM POSITIVE!

JUNE 2

Accepting personal responsibility is not saying "my bad" after something doesn't work out. When you truly accept personal responsibility for the outcome you will never say "my bad" again.

I AM POSITIVE!

JUNE 3

I cannot believe I am saying this out loud; however, there is a huge benefit if you really connect to the message. Okay, here goes, "Rules are for unaware people." What I mean is if you are living a normal, boring, predictable life, then I suggest that your new rule is to break a few rules. Besting your best may require you to color outside the lines and take a few risks. If you have the courage to take this on, you may find that a brand new possibility to recreate excellence just might occur.

I AM POSITIVE!

JUNE 4

Whether you are a positive thinker or a negative thinker, your thoughts ultimately will produce your results. If you do not like the results of your thoughts, change them.

I AM POSITIVE!

JUNE 5

I know you are in a hurry to get this incredible
day started so I will be quick. What is the space
between "what if" and "if only" called?
You got it, "missed opportunity". Life is not a
dress rehearsal, this is your NOW!
Create an amazing day!!!

I AM POSITIVE!

JUNE 6

If you want something you have never had, you must
be willing to do something you have never done.
Until you have the courage to risk success and take
that leap, you will never know what incredible wings you
can build, and you will never know what it feels like to fly.
Okay, so here we go. Set a positive outcome, something
that makes your heart race, something that makes
your palms sweat, something that makes you feel
butterflies in your tummy. YES! That's it! Now go for it.

I AM POSITIVE!

JUNE 7

If common sense is so common, then why is it so rare?
There are very few facts; however, there is a ton of
common sense and personal interpretations. If you
continue to hold on to your common sense and
interpretations as if they are facts, I will predict that
you will experience conflict in your relationships.
If you continue to do that, the only benefit you will
receive is when all has been said and done you will
get to be right. How is that working for you?

I AM POSITIVE!

JUNE 8

The greatest challenge you will ever face in life will come from within. Every outcome that you create in life has an origin... it has a starting point where it begins and where it manifests from. That point of origin is within you, within the conversation that you are creating in every given moment. It is in that internal moment that your outcome becomes possible. It is given strength and life and allowed to grow, or it becomes impossible, shrouded in doubt and fear. Tough circumstances may present themselves in this journey of life, and it is from within you, within that conversation, that you create the energy of defeat or victory. It always begins with you. Once you become present to this truth... the possibilities are endless, and the challenges become merely one more step forward.

I AM POSITIVE!

JUNE 9

In order to grow as a leader, you must be willing to grow as a person. Every last one of us occupies the largest room in the house, and that is the room for improvement. Now, I understand that personal growth is the toughest kind of growth there is, YAY YAY. That must mean that it produces the greatest benefit there is. Sounds like it is worth taking the risk to grow. "Grow for it".

I AM POSITIVE!

JUNE 10

Attitudes are contagious, whether they are positive or negative. Don't wait to catch your attitude from others, choose to infect every environment you are in with a positive attitude. Every time that happens it started with one person; why not you, why not NOW? It is important to know that the biggest energy in any environment will prevail.

I AM POSITIVE!

JUNE 11

I have a challenge for you this morning. Go out and catch five people doing something right today. Okay, well you really only need to find four people because I recommend that you start by catching yourself doing something right today.
This is going to be fun.

I AM POSITIVE!

JUNE 12

I will share my top 5 tips to create a powerful, positive day.
Here are the first two today; the rest are on the way tomorrow.

TIP #1
Move your alarm clock across the room.
Make a commitment to yourself that when the
alarm goes off, you will get out of bed and stay up.
Every time you hit that snooze button, you are enrolled in
a negative conversation with yourself. You are beginning
the day by creating negativity that you must overcome.

TIP #2
The first thing I recommend you do after you get up
is to read something positive rather than reading the
newspaper or turning on the news to start your day. It is
predictable that the messages you get from the newspaper
and the news will be focused on negative things.

I AM POSITIVE!

JUNE 13

Here is part two of the tips to create a powerful, positive day.

TIP #3

Write down your positive outcomes for the day. How will you know if the choices you make today are appropriate or not? You must have an outcome set. No matter the circumstance, when you are outcome focused, you continue to move forward by remaining focused on your outcome. My motto is "iFOTO" (I Focus On The Outcome).

TIP #4

Take time to spend a few moments meditating and visualizing a positive, successful day. This does not need to take more than five minutes. You must first believe the things you want are possible and you must believe you are worthy of having them because you are.

TIP #5

Now it is party time. Find your favorite, positive, upbeat song and have a morning party. Celebrate the success you know will happen today. If you believe that your outcomes are imminent, then celebrate them now. Starting your day this way will create new possibilities for you every day. By the way, every day begins with a morning; you may want to fall in love with mornings.

I AM POSITIVE!

JUNE 14

Conducting an inventory of the people you have
surrounded yourself with will tell you a lot about yourself.
If those relationships are bringing positive energy to the
environment, keep'em; however, if they are bringing
negative energy to the environment, change'em.
Oh wait, what if you are the negative one?
Then it's time to change you. I'm just sayin'.

I AM POSITIVE!

JUNE 15

Have you ever wondered what the world would look like if everyone fought for what they wanted and nobody fought against what they did not want? What do you want? If the answer to that question does not increase your heart rate, it is too small. Dig deeper and let's make it happen.
Life is not a dress rehearsal.

I AM POSITIVE!

JUNE 16

If you want to find the culprit that is producing the reality you are experiencing right now, you need not look far. Yes, you guessed correctly, it is you. Check the conversation you are having with yourself because energy and action follow thought. If you don't like the results that conversation is producing, you must change the conversation in order to change the results.

I AM POSITIVE!

JUNE 17

Never confuse knowledge with wisdom.
Knowledge helps you make a living and wisdom
helps you make a life. There is a difference between
IQ and EQ, and the journey from one to the other is the
toughest journey you will ever make. The distance
seems short; however, the journey is long. Having the
courage to make that 14 inch journey from your head to
your heart enables you to experience life from a new
perspective. Taking that journey shifts the way
you see the world and creates a connection to your
relationships that enables you to truly live life on purpose!

I AM POSITIVE!

JUNE 18

Remember your attitude is not controlled by what is happening to you, however it is 100% controlled by the conversation you are having with yourself about what is happening to you. We should also note that every time an environment was infected by a negative attitude it also began with one person. Sounds like that "I am Personally Responsible" thing keeps showing up.

I AM POSITIVE!

JUNE 19

I have had the privilege of conducting hundreds of keynote speeches. It never fails that people tell me how motivated they were by the speech. I was wondering, "Why is it okay for us to be our greatest critic but it is not okay for us to be our greatest supporter?" I believe that motivation is a management tool and when we become self-motivated, we become self-managed. I am still not understanding why that is a problem. My coaching to you today is to give yourself a high five today.

I AM POSITIVE!

JUNE 20

Be aware that if you continue to believe that it is possible to make others what you think they should be, you will continue to experience disappointment. When you apply that same focus to yourself, there is a greater chance for success. I'm just sayin'.

I AM POSITIVE!

JUNE 21

If you find yourself repressing your feelings,
then there is a great likelihood you are living with
disappointment, frustration, stress and anger.
When you express your wants, needs and feelings,
at the very least you create a possibility that you
will receive those things. The one thing we are
certain about is that if you continue to repress
those things, you may never get what you want
and need from the people in your life. This just may
be the greatest gift you give to yourself and others.

I AM POSITIVE!

JUNE 22

We spend a lot of time in classrooms learning and gaining knowledge, and that is very important. However, it does not matter if you made straight A's; knowledge is only powerful when it is applied. Knowledge is knowing what to do; wisdom is being on purpose and knowing when to do it.

I AM POSITIVE!

JUNE 23

Wouldn't it be REALLY, REALLY cool to know that everything – I mean absolutely everything - is going to turn out just the way you thought it would? It will! Energy and action follow thought. Time to check that conversation you are having with yourself... are you focused on positive or negative?

I AM POSITIVE!

JUNE 24

There is a difference between the flag hanging on
a flag pole and the wind. The wind chooses its direction,
and acts upon everything in its environment. The flag,
on the other hand, waits to be acted upon and it waits for
direction to be given. Learn to set your course by the stars,
not by the lights of every passing ship. My coaching to
you is to focus on besting your best every day.
Shoot for the stars.

I AM POSITIVE!

JUNE 25

You are going to spend a lot of time with yourself. You may want to fall in love with yourself. You really are worth it.

I AM POSITIVE!

JUNE 26

You are greater than anything that has ever happened to you. You've got to understand that whatever happened, happened. This is not an invitation to get over anything; this is an invitation to get on with your life. It is the only one you will get.

I AM POSITIVE!

JUNE 27

This is your reminder that in order to
create unreasonable, positive, new possibilities you will
need to do things you have never done. Continuing to
start your day the way you always have will create
a predictable future. Most people start their day with
a negative; they hit the snooze button. Think about the
conversation you are having with yourself when you hit
the snooze button, is it positive or negative? Now that we
are clear about that, it is time to change that behavior.

I AM POSITIVE!

JUNE 28

You get to choose to be the flag or the wind.
The flag is passive and moves in the direction of the
strongest energy, in other words it waits for direction,
the wind chooses. A life on purpose is never boring,
empty or meaningless. A life on purpose is a CHOICE.
Choose it today and play full out.

I AM POSITIVE!

JUNE 29

I challenge you to transform something negative
into something positive today. When you do, in that
moment you will have invented a new future.
Now, if you choose to continue practicing this
every day, you will become an inventor.
How cool is that? Life is Great!

I AM POSITIVE!

JUNE 30

Your dreams, potential, and aspirations are your unreasonable, positive new possibilities. In order to manifest them in your life, you must first believe in the possibility of waking up and making your dreams a reality. There are no limitations or impossibilities; they only exist within your capacity to believe.
So check the conversation you are having with yourself.
If it is not the conversation that will get to what you want, change it, and watch what happens!

I AM POSITIVE!

JULY 1

You have likely received, and perhaps sent out a few invitations to some pity parties. I promise you, they are no fun and attending a pity party will only produce a negative outcome. Now that you have that awareness, my coaching to you is to not waste your time and energy feeling sorry for yourself and others because it will never benefit anyone. The sooner you refocus on your positive outcome, the sooner this party will become a celebration. It is PARTY TIME!!

I AM POSITIVE!

JULY 2

It is important that you set a positive academic, personal and professional outcome for your life. Articulate what the "BIG" picture looks like and keep in mind that your journey will only be accomplished one step at a time. It is not about how fast you get there, live in the moment and enjoy the journey.

I AM POSITIVE!

JULY 3

It does not matter in this moment what has happened to you. Whatever happened is history, the awareness I offer you today is if you remain focused on what happened, it will become your future. Whatever you focus on will continually expand for you. With that awareness, I encourage you to focus on what you want. Life is Great!

I AM POSITIVE!

JULY 4

It is possible for you to be the "Game Changer" in every professional and personal relationship you have. This will require you to be aware of a few things: take nothing personal, accept personal responsibility to get what you want from the relationship, never sell or buy tickets to a pity party, focus on the positive, and be flexible. Good Day, "Game Changer".

I AM POSITIVE!

JULY 5

Most people spend more time planning a two-week vacation than they spend planning for the rest of their lives. Be aware that this life is not a dress rehearsal. What will they say about you when you are gone? Your choices are writing the story of your life. My coaching to you is to write a best seller.

I AM POSITIVE!

JULY 6

Each of us has a personal MAP that was developed
by the humans who taught us everything they knew.
They didn't know everything; therefore, the highest
form of ignorance is to reject something just because
it's not on your MAP. Your MAP is not the entire territory;
it's just your MAP. Make the choice to learn one new
thing from someone today. If you do,
you will need a bigger MAP.

I AM POSITIVE!

JULY 7

Brand new opportunities are always there for you. So if opportunity doesn't come knocking at your door, open the door anyway and have the courage to go for what you want. Every journey begins with the first step. Whatever that step or action is... do it NOW!!

I AM POSITIVE!

JULY 8

Take a moment to compare the difference in the
energy of when you are running from something that
will potentially create pain to when you are running
to something that will potentially produce gain.
Set a positive outcome today and write down
five benefits you will receive when you accomplish it.
Focus on what you what, it feels good. Life is Great!

I AM POSITIVE!

JULY 9

When an individual has the courage to take a stand,
the spines of others are stiffened. It is not the critic who
counts; nor is it the person who points out how the doer
of courageous deeds could have done them better.
The credit belongs to the person who has the courage to
"get in the game" and give it heart, body and soul
focused on a positive outcome for themselves and others.
Take a stand for what you want today. You are worth it.

I AM POSITIVE!

JULY 10

You are cause in every reality in your life, not effect. There are no victims, only volunteers. So, WAYFO? (What Are You Focused On?) What you focus on will expand for you because energy and action follow thought. If you want to find the culprit that is producing the realities you are experiencing every second of the day, you need not look far. Check the conversation that you are having with yourself and the choices you are making. If you want to change your results, you must change the conversation you are having with yourself and the choices you are making.

I AM POSITIVE!

JULY 11

It is impossible to awaken a person who is pretending to be asleep. Many of us who have begun the journey of personal growth and self-awareness have gained insight and knowledge about ourselves that we did not have prior to having the courage to take that journey. You must continue learning and growing because this stuff is real simple; however, it is not easy. You must practice new learnings and behaviors daily because knowledge is only powerful when it is applied.

I AM POSITIVE!

JULY 12

Some people compare personal growth to a marathon saying things like "It's a journey". That is a someday conversation. Learning and growing is a CHOICE, you get to choose to do it or not in this present moment. I agree that personal growth is a journey, so if you need to compare it to something, let's call it a sprint.
It is okay to TAN (Take Action Now)!

I AM POSITIVE!

JULY 13

The greatest determiners of your happiness and success is not your circumstances, rather it is your assessment of the circumstances. There is positive and negative in EVERYTHING. WAYFO? (What Are You Focused On?) Success and happiness will not happen to you, it will happen because of you.

I AM POSITIVE!

JULY 14

Every one of us occupies the largest room in the house and that is the room for improvement. Everyone you meet knows something that you do not. Choose to redefine your personal 100% daily by being willing to learn from them. Open your mind and heart and fill some of that space.

I AM POSITIVE!

JULY 15

Take a moment to identify a few of the little things
you are allowing to irritate or annoy you today.
Once you have identified them ask yourself this
question, "How will that benefit me today?"
Hmmm, that's what I thought. You may just want
to let that little stuff go, because it is robbing
you of joy, peace and happiness.

I AM POSITIVE!

JULY 16

I have a simple little thought to share with you today that will make a big difference. The only people you should ever want to get "even" with are those who have given to you and influenced you in a positive way. So I have some homework for you today, take a moment to write down just five positive things that have happened to you because of someone else, now Pay it Forward! Wow, is that a smile on your face? Didn't that feel good?

I AM POSITIVE!

JULY 17

I have heard it said, "There is a time to lead and a time to follow." I completely disagree with that concept. I believe that you should always be a leader. Now this submits that you should always be your own boss, and accept responsibility for every choice you are making regarding your behavior at ALL times. Always being a leader comes with the understanding there are no victims in the context of this conversation, only volunteers.

I AM POSITIVE!

JULY 18

There is an "i" in team! IT'S YOU! You matter, you count. You will affect the outcome of everything you do either positively or negatively. If you think you are too small or your position is insignificant to make a difference, then you have never been in bed with a mosquito.

I AM POSITIVE!

JULY 19

I am often asked, "When do you possibly have time to spend with your four sons?" Well, what I have learned and committed to over the years is to make sure that the time I spend with my family is more focused on quality and not quantity. It is my belief that when the game of life is over for you, it will not matter what the score is on the score board, what will matter most, is how you played the game.

I AM POSITIVE!

JULY 20

Sir Winston Churchill once said, "If you're going through hell, keep going." Going through challenging circumstances is the worst time to stop moving. Keep pushing, focused on a positive outcome, and you will gain the confidence to break through the challenge.

I AM POSITIVE!

JULY 21

In my book entitled, Change Your Mind, Change Your World, I talk about the difference between being the flag and the wind. The flag represents people who live their lives as victims waiting for someone to give them permission to live. Every time a strong wind comes along they find themselves moving in the direction of the strongest wind. An effective leader is the wind. They define ahead of time what they want, what they stand for, and what they will do. There are no victims, only volunteers, and excuses are for losers. Set your course today; life is not a dress rehearsal.

(By the way, you can get a copy of the book at www.discoverleadership.com)

I AM POSITIVE!

JULY 22

When you take a step, you travel about 3 feet
in distance. People often say, "Go the extra mile."
My coaching to you today is to go the extra 3 feet;
take the next step.

I AM POSITIVE!

JULY 23

Enthusiasm is a form of excitement and it is contagious. As children, we had unbridled enthusiasm and for many of us the flame was slowly put out. Be aware you cannot light a fire with a wet match. Make the choice to reignite your fire of enthusiasm today and set your environment ablaze. It will only take one person to have the courage to create this opportunity. Why not you, why not now? It's not too late to recapture the zest for life you had as a child, because it's never too late to have a happy childhood. Life is Great!

I AM POSITIVE!

JULY 24

The best way to forget your problems is to help someone else solve theirs. When you give, it always comes back to you. It may not look like what you gave; however, it will come back to you, because Givers Gain. There is need ALL around you. Give someone a gift today and enrich their life. It could be as simple as catching someone doing something "right" and smiling at someone. Make the world a better place today because of you.
Life is Great!

I AM POSITIVE!

JULY 25

When you declare with passion and enthusiasm
that NOTHING is impossible for you and you truly
believe it, you will attain everything you desire.

I AM POSITIVE!

JULY 26

I am saddened by the number of people who play small
or play not to lose. Complaining about what you do not have
or blaming someone else for not providing it for you will
never positively benefit you. The time has come for you to
understand that no one owes you a living or anything else.
What you accomplish in your life is up to you.
If there is no wind to assist you in getting to your
destination, then row. If the path is not clear leading to
where you want to go, then create it. If you do not have
the resources to get what you want, then obtain them.
If you are committed to getting what you want,
then make it happen.

I AM POSITIVE!

JULY 27

Focusing on the things that went wrong yesterday creates
depression. Focusing on things that could go wrong
tomorrow creates anxiety. The greatest gift that you
have is choice, so choose to focus on this present moment!
Give everything you have to making positive memories
in the moment that will produce a likeness of itself.

I AM POSITIVE!

JULY 28

As you focus on getting everything that life has to offer you today, I encourage you to go for it; however, there is no need for you to prevent anyone else from doing the same.

I AM POSITIVE!

JULY 29

Have you ever given someone what you felt like were
perfect instructions and they got it ALL wrong?
Okay, that has likely NEVER happened to you; however,
it has happened to a few of us. When it does happen
to you, I have a little coaching that will help you,
blaming them for what went wrong will not resolve it.
If the approach you are using to convey your message
is not working – change it!

I AM POSITIVE!

JULY 30

The only person you should compare yourself to is you. Are you besting your best today? In this moment, you are either green and growing or you are dying and decaying, there is no neutral. Stay focused on your outcome and driven by the benefits of that outcome. Remember to measure your progress!

I AM POSITIVE!

JULY 31

A lit candle loses absolutely nothing by lighting another candle. Holding on to your gifts and talents has no benefit; give them away. When you give your gifts away, it is a win/win situation. What gift will you give away today?

I AM POSITIVE!

AUGUST

AUGUST 1

Ability is what you're capable of doing, so
focus on increasing your capacity every day.
Motivation determines what you do and as long
as it is internal, you will continue doing it. Attitude
determines how well you will choose to do it, so slap
on a smile and have fun doing whatever you
are focused on today.

I AM POSITIVE!

AUGUST 2

I agree that you are ONLY one person; however, whatever you do today will matter, so do something positive. Hmmm...nuff said.

I AM POSITIVE!

AUGUST 3

What are you clinging to from your past that is
preventing you from moving forward?
When you open your grip and let that slip away what
you are really doing is allowing room for something
brand new to occur in your life. Okay, let's do that today.

I AM POSITIVE!

AUGUST 4

I encourage you to go for the things you really want
in your life. Never believe that you have failed or lost.
It is not over until you say it is over.

I AM POSITIVE!

AUGUST 5

I came across something really important and wanted to share it with you. It appears that this personal development thing has some real benefit. Research now shows that an employee's performance will move 30% positively in environments where there is a commitment to personal development and 30% negatively in environments that are not committed to personal development. I know what you are thinking, I had the same thought... this information coming from me is like a nutritionist commenting on the value of healthy eating. Hmmm, you may want to take a look at that.

I AM POSITIVE!

AUGUST 6

I'm sure you will agree that no one can live your life for you. And yet, so often, we indeed let others control our life by making choices that will please them and allow them to feel safe or make them look good. Why would you do this? How will it benefit you in a positive way? I would really like to hear the conversation you are having with yourself regarding this.

I AM POSITIVE!

AUGUST 7

The way your life is right now is nothing more than the manifestation of your choices. There are no victims, only volunteers. Make sure the choices you are making will manifest the outcomes you want. If you are blaming something or someone else, the game is over, and there is no chance you will succeed. Only when you accept personal responsibility do you keep what's possible alive.

I AM POSITIVE!

AUGUST 8

To paraphrase the wisdom of Kenny Rogers, you have to know when to hold'em, know when to fold'em, know when to walk away, and know when to run like hell. So here is a POA (Plan Of Action) to practice today, "Be in the Moment." Nuff said.

I AM POSITIVE!

AUGUST 9

When you have belief, faith, and courage;
everything that you want has a great chance
of becoming your reality.

I AM POSITIVE!

AUGUST 10

Become aware of the conversation you are having with yourself. If your best friend was having that conversation with you would he remain your best friend or would you be finding a new friend? Make sure the conversations you are having with yourself reflect the kind of friend that will benefit you. Make a commitment to yourself to love and be kind to yourself.

I AM POSITIVE!

AUGUST 11

When you get to the edge of your comfort zone today and get that feeling to step back into its safety, remind yourself that the thought of safety is just an illusion and instead of keeping you safe it's holding you back. Step powerfully through the edge of that comfort zone and keep going after what you really, really want. You gotta bring something to this in order to get something from it!!

I AM POSITIVE!

AUGUST 12

Take time today to exercise the 80 muscles in your face.
Do some "up downs". A laugh is never a foreign language
to anyone, and a smile speaks all languages.
It's a GREAT day to be alive!

I AM POSITIVE!

AUGUST 13

I have often told people that energy and action
follow thought. So with that in mind, if you feel that
you are one of those people that is snake bitten, you
have a dark cloud over your head, and everything
you touch turns sour -- my coaching to you is to not go
sky diving until you get that worked out. I'm just sayin'.

I AM POSITIVE!

AUGUST 14

There are a lot of people leaving butt prints in the sands of time while sitting on the sidelines waiting for life to happen to them, and yet there are others that are following the path created by someone else. Someone will have the courage to create a brand new path for others to follow that will bring even more value to the quality of life. Why not YOU? Why not NOW?

I AM POSITIVE!

AUGUST 15

I have often heard individuals wishing each other "good luck" when faced with a task or challenge to complete. I have not been able to determine where this "good luck" comes from or who the caretaker of it is. Is it the same person that sends the "bad luck"? Well, if you get that figured out, please share it with me because my truth is, luck (whether good or bad) will not determine the ultimate outcome. You will. I'm just sayin'.

I AM POSITIVE!

AUGUST 16

Notice today how often you make someone wrong
so that you can be right. What's the benefit in that?
They don't have to be wrong for you to be right.
This now creates a win/win instead of a win/lose.
Be the game changer by choosing to accept
people for who they choose to be!

I AM POSITIVE!

AUGUST 17

Dead fish go with the current, but it takes a live fish
to go against the current. So CHOOSE to be ALIVE and
CREATE AN UNREASONABLE POSSIBILITY TODAY!!

I AM POSITIVE!

AUGUST 18

In every one of us is a child that would love to come out and play. The only reason we get old is because we stop playing. Have a little fun today.

I AM POSITIVE!

AUGUST 19

Rather than focusing on all of the circumstances and people in your life that need to change to make you happy, simply choose to be happy. Be aware that the common denominator in every one of those situations is you. I'm just sayin'.

I AM POSITIVE!

AUGUST 20

It is predictable that an amazing, negative, positive, worst day of my life, horrible, best day ever, good, great day is going to happen in the next 24 hours. It is also predictable that the day you choose will be your reality today. Wow, did you know you had that much control over what kind of day you had? Allow that thought to percolate and marinate for a little while.

I AM POSITIVE!

AUGUST 21

I believe that the greatest wisdom is gained when we are quiet. The answers that you seek are in the silence. It's a little early for such a deep thought, so it's okay to save it until this afternoon.

I AM POSITIVE!

AUGUST 22

I have had the pleasure of coaching a few
great men and women and I found that the people
who are more successful, are those who were in the
moment and did whatever was necessary to get to
their outcome. I also observed they gave everything
they had to get to their outcome.

I AM POSITIVE!

AUGUST 23

Everything you see today is not necessarily all there is to see. Quite often, the way we see things through our lens, is connected to our "BS" (Belief System) and how we see ourselves. So if you change the way you are looking at things, those things will change. I recommend that your plan of action today should focus on "being in the moment".

I AM POSITIVE!

AUGUST 24

Once you set a course to the positive outcomes you want in your professional and personal lives, remain focused on your outcome. The winds will blow and the waves will pound the boat, however, stay the course. If the sea was always calm, you could never practice your navigational skills.

I AM POSITIVE!

AUGUST 25

It is so important to give your 100% every time in everything you do; however, it is important to be aware that it has its limitations. There is so much more that can be accomplished through the synergy of a powerful team. Synergistic teamwork divides the task and multiplies the success - sounds like there could be a professional and personal application from this thought. I'm just sayin'.

I AM POSITIVE!

AUGUST 26

I want to help you with an awareness today that just may change the way you see everything and everyone you encounter today. Everything you are viewing or experiencing on any level is going through your personal filter. You are assessing if those things are good, attractive, ugly, bad or whatever. Okay, here is the awareness, the assessments you make have nothing to do with your feelings or moods relating to what you see, you are creating 100% of them based on your personal map. And here is an even bigger awareness ... your map is not the entire territory - it is just your map.

I AM POSITIVE!

AUGUST 27

I've got a question as you begin this day...
If you are not committed to play full out today,
why play at all? Just a little reminder,
life is not a dress rehearsal.

I AM POSITIVE!

AUGUST 28

The greatest barrier to success is the fear of failure.
Some say that the person who believes they "can" win,
will win. That is not necessarily so because I "can" is
nothing more than a statement of potential.
Let's go next level, the person who commits they
"will win" has a greater chance of succeeding.
I'm just sayin'.

I AM POSITIVE!

AUGUST 29

Continually asking yourself, "What else will I do to get to my outcome?" allows you to move through circumstances quickly. Blaming others only serves to keep you stuck. So, who will you choose to be today to get to your outcomes?

I AM POSITIVE!

AUGUST 30

Too often we see problems as problems.
So, we avoid them, hide them, and pretend we
don't have any problems. Well, the things that we
refer to as problems are actually gifts.
They provide us with an opportunity to live,
learn, and grow. Now really, is that a problem?

I AM POSITIVE!

AUGUST 31

When you become angry or frustrated, harness that energy and redirect it to something positive. It takes a lot of unnecessary energy and effort to eliminate anger and frustration; instead, treat them as gifts.

I AM POSITIVE!

SEPTEMBER

SEPTEMBER 1

I have heard a large number of people over the years say, "You can't teach an old dog new tricks." I said to a few of those "old dogs" that it is okay to develop a habit around catching people doing things right rather than always catching them doing things wrong. Their response, "I never thought about that." Mission accomplished.

I AM POSITIVE!

SEPTEMBER 2

Purpose is love made visible, so I have a few tough
questions for you today. Who are you?
Why are you here on this earth? What do you stand for?
What positive difference is your life making?
Did you know that you are a very important person?
Okay, now that you do, we need you to get the rest figured
out. If you need some help with this, I have your back.

I AM POSITIVE!

SEPTEMBER 3

You may be disappointed if you fail; however, you are doomed to fail if you never take the first step. There is one prevailing factor that keeps individuals stuck in their rut, planted on the sidelines, and watching life pass them by - that is fear...fear of the unknown, fear of change, fear of failure, fear of taking a risk. There is a good reason I am bringing this to your attention today. I had a friend that recently died at 31 years old. I assure you, she never thought that 15 years old was middle age... this life is not a dress rehearsal - it is okay to live it out loud and on purpose NOW!!!! Unless you have the courage to take that first step, you may never know what successes are possible for you.

I AM POSITIVE!

SEPTEMBER 4

People love to send their team members to our programs believing they "need" them. The truth is, no one "needs" to attend our programs; however, everyone deserves to receive the benefits of our programs.

I AM POSITIVE!

SEPTEMBER 5

I have heard so many people say, "I will forgive you, however I will not forget." Well, okay let's speak some truth here; that really is just another way of saying, "I will not forgive you." True forgiveness is like blowing up a bridge. There is nothing to go back to, it is finished. You will never get a positive return by holding on to anything that is negative. Just a thought, blow up the bridge and get on with your life. It is the only life you get.

I AM POSITIVE!

SEPTEMBER 6

A coward gets scared whenever circumstances out of the norm show up, and they quit. A hero also gets scared, however, they keep moving forward, no matter what, until they succeed. Did you know that you get to choose to be a coward or a hero?

I AM POSITIVE!

SEPTEMBER 7

A reporter once asked me why I believe that anything is possible. I told him that my mom and dad told me that it was and I believed them. As a result, I have accomplished things in my life that others have felt were impossible. If you believe you can, you will. Okay, let's get this handled today.

I AM POSITIVE!

SEPTEMBER 8

In this present moment I strongly encourage you to destroy, crush, and kill every fear you encounter in others and in yourself. Fear is a gift provided to you for the sole purpose of building your courage muscle. Build some big courage muscles today. Focus on unreasonable positive possibilities.

I AM POSITIVE!

SEPTEMBER 9

If you remain tied to the pains of the past, the future is predictable. I have a suggestion for you today. The future can also be predictable if you set a positive outcome and commit to creating the future you want. Isn't it cool how that works?

I AM POSITIVE!

SEPTEMBER 10

Every challenging situation is an opportunity for significant positive personal growth. Take a moment to grieve the loss, then get on with it, you are worth it.

I AM POSITIVE!

SEPTEMBER 11

What would it be like to love like you have never been hurt,
let down, or betrayed before? I knew you would say that.
Tell you what, let's go for it and find out. This is not a
conversation about getting over anything or anyone;
it is however, a conversation about getting on with it.

I AM POSITIVE!

SEPTEMBER 12

There is a team member that will need this today - SMILE. Did you just realize it was you? I can be a little sneaky sometimes. LOL!

I AM POSITIVE!

SEPTEMBER 13

Apprehension only exists in the conversation you
are having with yourself. Stand up to your fears -
you will find that they are not as strong as
you thought they were.

I AM POSITIVE!

SEPTEMBER 14

The behaviors that you are practicing today, are those behaviors you will become the MASTER of. Every choice matters.

I AM POSITIVE!

SEPTEMBER 15

There is a tremendous number of people who are still searching high and low for their purpose in life. I am not sure how high or how low you have looked for your purpose, however, the reason you didn't find your purpose there, is because it is not there. Your purpose is within you.

I AM POSITIVE!

SEPTEMBER 16

It has been said that living your life on purpose is like having six in one hand and half a dozen in the other; it really doesn't matter. Do you think they really believe that, or is the real message "I am afraid to get out of my comfort zone"?

I AM POSITIVE!

SEPTEMBER 17

As you travel this journey of personal growth, you will encounter many roadblocks, obstacles, circumstances, and huge walls. Let the celebration begin because we now get an opportunity to authenticate the work that we have been doing. You better get clear as it relates to who has your back.

I AM POSITIVE!

SEPTEMBER 18

My coaching to you today is to stay away from negative people who belittle your ambitions. Small people always do that, the really great people make you feel that you, too, can become great. Getting to your next level of leadership development will be challenging, embrace the challenge. In order to create something you've never created, you must conquer the challenge.

I AM POSITIVE!

SEPTEMBER 19

For true, sustainable success in your life, continually ask yourself, "What else will I do to get to the success I want in my personal and professional relationships?" When you realize an answer, have the courage to make it happen and give up the need to be "right".

I AM POSITIVE!

SEPTEMBER 20

Generally, when we use absolutes in our communications (always, never), we are coming from emotion and it's predictable that the drama is about to show up. When we are coming from emotion, we are not communicating effectively. My coaching is to check the conversation you are having with yourself and address what is making you emotional before talking about anything else. I'm just sayin'.

I AM POSITIVE!

SEPTEMBER 21

As you set and focus on your outcome, you must be willing to take the steps necessary to manifest that outcome. There will be certain circumstances along your journey that you have no control over, and as you encounter these circumstances, you have the option of either reacting or responding. Our plan of action for TODAY is to be in the moment.

I AM POSITIVE!

SEPTEMBER 22

There are many factors that individuals rely upon to create success. They rest back on the laurels of their talent, strength, power, intelligence, education, and position. The one determining factor that will outlast each of these factors is your perseverance. Constantly moving forward - focused on the outcome - will create your push, your growth, and ultimately your success. Persevere in creating what you want... YOU make the difference!

I AM POSITIVE!

SEPTEMBER 23

When was the last time you fell flat on your butt?
Well, if it wasn't yesterday, it is time to get out of that
comfort zone. What looks like failure is nothing more
than a precursor to success, as long as you stay in the
game. If you fall down five times, stand up six.
By the way, it is okay to surround yourself with a
few positive cheerleaders.

I AM POSITIVE!

SEPTEMBER 24

How happy are you at this point in your life?
What else do you feel that you need to be happier?
I submit that many of us look for happiness in how
successful we have been in the events of life.
Successful events are not the key to happiness;
choosing to be happy will be the key to your success.

I AM POSITIVE!

SEPTEMBER 25

There is a level in this game at which few are willing to play. The greatest differentiating factor for individuals at this level is that they are willing to accept PERSONAL RESPONSIBILITY. Making the choice to accept personal responsibility is to have an understanding that you ARE responsible... for who you are, for your happiness, for your fulfillment, for your success, for your focus, for your positivity, for your enthusiasm, and for living your purpose. YOU are responsible - you are who you are, because you choose to be.

I AM POSITIVE!

SEPTEMBER 26

The way people treat you is the way you have TAUGHT them to treat you. You are in control of how you project yourself to the world. How you react or respond in certain situations, the value you give to the people around you, the behaviors you encourage or allow from them, and the boundaries you create, all affect how individuals will BE with you. If you are looking for a different result in how someone is treating you, change your approach with them to create something different.

I AM POSITIVE!

SEPTEMBER 27

Living a life on purpose means having the courage to go after the things that you really want. As you continue to stretch yourself, new possibilities open up and you begin to experience life in a bigger way. Playing it safe and living on the sidelines boxes you in and limits your possibilities AND your potential. The amazing connection to make is that the choice is yours. You can choose - in THIS moment - t
o have courage. Go BIG or go home!

I AM POSITIVE!

SEPTEMBER 28

Have you ever thought of yourself as a salesperson?
Every conversation or interaction we have is a
sales transaction and somebody is being sold
something during every one of those transactions.
What are you buying and what are you selling?
If you are unsure, check your attitude.
The answer is being stored there.

I AM POSITIVE!

SEPTEMBER 29

Do you believe you have a life purpose?
Do you believe you can choose one?
The journey starts right now, and it is 14 inches
long from your head to your heart. Follow your
heart in everything you do, and you'll never
be without purpose - or joy, or abundance,
or love, or happiness... I'll bet you never
saw that coming.

I AM POSITIVE!

SEPTEMBER 30

It's OKAY to TAN (Take Action Now). This is a choice you get to make every day of your life. You can remain on the sidelines, playing it safe, doing the same thing you've always done and getting the same results; however, in doing this, you will also get the opportunity to experience the leftovers in the wake of those who are in the game. Aren't you worth more than that? Take the steps to get in the game and "BE" the one blazing the trail, holding nothing back, creating Unreasonable Possibilities, and living your life on purpose. TAN!

I AM POSITIVE!

OCTOBER 1

If you hear a voice within you saying "you cannot win",
and you choose to stay on the sidelines, you will not win.
Silence that voice and get in the game. The only person
controlling the conversation you're having with yourself
is YOU. That conversation creates the results you
produce in your life, both positive and negative.
You are 100% personally responsible for those results.
Push through your fears, self-doubt, and apprehension
and just TAN (Take Action Now)!

I AM POSITIVE!

OCTOBER 2

There is a difference between being focused on the
outcome and being attached to the outcome. Truly
being focused on the outcome means giving your 100% to
manifest that outcome, creating the conversation and the
behavior that will bring you closer to that outcome, and
understanding there are things outside your control that
could affect whether you reach that outcome or not.
Being attached to the outcome will lead to frustration
and disappointment if the outcome is not met - despite
the existence of things outside your control.
Realize that all you can control is your own give
and your own attitude in the midst of that give.
Let go of any attachment to how it turns out.

I AM POSITIVE!

OCTOBER 3

Each of us reproduces a likeness of our self, whether you maintain a positive attitude or a negative attitude - whether you are self-confidence or have a lack of self-confidence or whether you are enthusiastic or lethargic. Whether you choose to live or just exist, then that is exactly what you will reproduce in the people around you in both your professional and personal life. Well, like it or not YOU are a Role Model.

I AM POSITIVE!

OCTOBER 4

Anything that keeps you from growing is never worth "right fighting" to defend. We all occupy the largest room in the house... and that is the room for improvement. Having an attitude of growth and learning means that we first make the choice to be OPEN to the learning. When an individual in your life has an offering, and you hear criticism or judgment, your defenses come up and you prepare for the fight. It is no longer an opportunity to grow the relationship; it now becomes a battlefield where you will go toe to toe to defend your position. At the end of the day, you will get to be "right". How is that working for you?

I AM POSITIVE!

OCTOBER 5

Regardless of what life has given you - whatever situations, circumstances, or events you are experiencing - you can ALWAYS choose to be unreasonable and go for what you want. There are no victims, only volunteers. One of the greatest gifts you have been given is choice and you can choose to create whatever reality you want. Despite what is going on around you, your attitude and your choices are still your own. Being unreasonable is redefined in every moment, so make the choice to create what you want... no reasons... no excuses... no alibis.

I AM POSITIVE!

OCTOBER 6

You are REALLY going to need to pay attention while reading this. Okay, here we go. Think of life from the perspective that there is no bad or good, it is all about the assessment you place on that situation based on your expectations. When you stop making those assessments based on your judgments, you become powerful because you will become aware that life only has the meaning you give it.

I AM POSITIVE!

OCTOBER 7

I apologize if this unromanticizes what love means to you; however, I believe this thought will create a new possibility for you to love more completely. I submit that love is a gift, available for you to give to anyone you want. My definition of love is accepting a person for who they are, and for who they aren't. So it is okay to love the folks in your life the way they want to be loved; if you don't know what that means, ask them. Oh, and by the way, rather than waiting for them to figure out how to love you the way you want to be loved, tell them.

I AM POSITIVE!

OCTOBER 8

It is impossible to awaken someone who is pretending to be asleep. We get at least two choices in life everyday - tough or suffering. We choose tough when we choose to play the game "Full Out" with no attachment to how it turns out. We choose suffering when we choose to stand on the sidelines in fear, watching life pass us by.
Well, that is only going to happen once.
I'm thinking it's not a good idea.

I AM POSITIVE!

OCTOBER 9

So many people continue looking outside of themselves for their purpose, however, it is inside of you. If that didn't make it more clear then this likely will. Decide what you are committed to do to leave this world better after you are gone. Guess what you just discovered? That's right, it's your purpose. Now move your butt and go make it happen!

I AM POSITIVE!

OCTOBER 10

Are you planning on having a great or crappy day today?
Whichever you choose will be your reality.
You did know that, right? Okay, let's be clear about this,
there will be a few things that happen today that you
will have NO control of; however, you will have
100% control over how you react to them.
Your reaction will create a systemic chain of events
that will then determine whether this will be
a Great Day or a crappy day.

I AM POSITIVE!

OCTOBER 11

The choices you make create your destiny.
Your destiny is not a fixed state of being.
Set a positive outcome today and continue
moving forward, making powerful and positive
choices in the direction of that outcome.
You can have what you want.
Believe it, because you are worth it.

I AM POSITIVE!

OCTOBER 12

Stop wasting your energy attempting to control situations and other people. The only thing this will lead to is frustration, disappointment, and anger. My best coaching to you in this moment is to STOP IT.

I AM POSITIVE!

OCTOBER 13

If you have an outcome set and there is no wind, then row.
The road to your outcome is not always paved. Sometimes,
it is NEVER paved. It is up to you to create the momentum
to overcome the inertia and keep moving forward.
Waiting around for conditions to be "perfect" before
taking action results in stagnancy; it results in you waiting
on the sidelines. Get off the sidelines and find the solution.

I AM POSITIVE!

OCTOBER 14

Self-worth cannot be verified by others. You are worthy because you say that it is so. Energy and action follow thought. You create the reality that you operate in based on the conversation you are having with yourself. If you give more value to what others think about you, then you are waiting on the sidelines... for their approval, for their assessment, and for their permission to live your life. There is no individual on this earth that can give YOU self-worth. It will only come from you.

I AM POSITIVE!

OCTOBER 15

Throw your heart into the game and the rest will follow.
Life is a game, accept it or not. You can choose to get in the game
or sit on the sidelines observing the game. If you choose to get in
the game, you can either play not to lose, or you can play to win.
I recommend that you choose to play full out, focused on
the win-win because life is not a dress rehearsal.

I AM POSITIVE!

OCTOBER 16

Do not wait until the iron is hot; but make it hot by striking! Face it - nobody owes you anything. What you do, or fail to do, is directly related to your choices. The time to make your dreams reality is NOW. How, you ask? Choose it.

I AM POSITIVE!

OCTOBER 17

There will come a day when each of us will be on our deathbed and, unfortunately, in that moment most people will be asking one question and making one statement: "What if" and "If only". This is your NOW, make the choice to play full out.

I AM POSITIVE!

OCTOBER 18

You may not believe this; however, there are people out there that are afraid of others' opinions and thoughts. In my opinion, this is the greatest sign of ignorance. If everybody has the same opinion, then somebody is not expressing theirs. It is comfortable, even easy, to live your life on the sidelines, maintaining the status quo and doing what is "reasonable". It is when you step away from the crowd and get in the game that you become distinct, that you begin to push up against the paradigm, and that you dare to be "unreasonable". Ultimately, diversity of thought brings more value, so make the choice to get in the game.

I AM POSITIVE!

OCTOBER 19

A very simple thought, however it makes a world of difference: if you focus on the difficulty in every opportunity, you will only see difficulty. If you focus on the opportunity in every difficulty, you will only see opportunity.
WAYFO? (What Are You Focused On?)

I AM POSITIVE!

OCTOBER 20

Talk is cheap because supply is over abundant and demand is low. Now is the time to stop talking about everything that is going wrong and focusing on "what ifs" or "woulda, coulda, shouldas". Make a commitment to yourself in this present moment to start working toward the things you want. Take Action Now (TAN) toward your outcomes. Every journey begins with the first step, so take that step NOW.
Life is not a dress rehearsal my friend.

I AM POSITIVE!

OCTOBER 21

It doesn't matter if you are a genius intellectually,
because knowledge and intelligence are both
useless without the courage to Take Action Now (TAN).
There is a huge difference in knowing how to do
something and having the courage to go for it
with your heart, body, and soul. Every one of us
will die one day, however, very few of us
will choose to live full out.

I AM POSITIVE!

OCTOBER 22

Take a look in the mirror - the person you see and the experiences you have had are the result of your choices. The choices you have made are to the things you were the most committed to. That can be an invigorating or a scary awareness.

I AM POSITIVE!

OCTOBER 23

As soon as you begin developing plan "B",
focused on what you will do after you do not
succeed at accomplishing your outcome,
you will have created a predictable future.
Come on, what is that about? Energy and
action follows thought, so take a look at what
you are thinking. If you are not committed
to plan "A" go back to the drawing board.

I AM POSITIVE!

OCTOBER 24

You don't know what you don't know until you know that you don't know. Okay, let's be real, none of us knows everything. Many of us believe that "If they know I don't know, I will die." Well, every one of us occupies the largest room in the house and that is the room for improvement. You will not grow professionally or personally until you accept that fact.

I AM POSITIVE!

OCTOBER 25

Here, at Discover Leadership Training, we believe that you manage things and you lead people. Therefore, management is a matter of routines, processes, accurate calculations, and statistics. Management is a science. Leadership is a matter of personal responsibility, commitment, courage and vision. Leadership is an art. Managers are necessary. Leaders are essential.

I AM POSITIVE!

OCTOBER 26

You are cause in the matter, not effect.
There are no victims, only volunteers, so what are
you focused on (WAYFO) in this present moment?
What you focus on will expand for you, because energy
and action follow thought. If you want to find the culprit
that is producing the outcomes you are experiencing
every second of the day you need not look far.
Check the conversation that you are having
with yourself. If you want to change your results,
you must change the conversation you are
having with yourself.

I AM POSITIVE!

OCTOBER 27

My absolute favorite Bible verse says, "You will know them by their fruit." There are a lot of people who "talk" a good game and others who "do" a lot of stuff to create an illusion of who they are. Who you "BE", the fruit that you produce in every given moment, is the real you and it's who they will become. Your fruit is either green and growing or ripe and decaying. Who are you choosing to be today and how is that choice affecting the world around you? You are affecting the outcome... you matter!

I AM POSITIVE!

OCTOBER 28

I've read that when you seek, you will find.
Okay, now that you've found what you want, what's next?
It will still require courage to make it happen.
No need to seek that! It is available right now.
Live today like you were dying.

I AM POSITIVE!

OCTOBER 29

Be sure to read the thought today very carefully,
this one is REALLY important. You are not a victim of
circumstance, you are a volunteer of circumstance.
Everyday circumstances occur in our lives.
Some of which we have absolutely no control over;
however, no matter the circumstance, we always
maintain control of our choices. Choose well my
friend, because your reality will be the result.

I AM POSITIVE!

OCTOBER 30

Winners lose much more often than losers, because winners take more risks to achieve what they really want. Oh wait.... since most winners choose to learn and grow from their losses they actually rarely lose. Every day we get to make a choice to get in the game or sit on the sidelines of life. Unfortunately most people blame the weather, the economy, the color of their skin, their age and many other things for not taking the risk to succeed. Yes, I said the risk to succeed. When you are focused on what you want, you are not risking failure, you are risking success, When you play full out, focused on success there is no failure.

I AM POSITIVE!

OCTOBER 31

As long as you have dreams, tomorrow has hope. As long as you have hope, new possibilities await you. Living your life on purpose is not about waiting for the storms to pass. This is your NOW. So whenever you get the chance to sit it out or dance, choose to dance.

I AM POSITIVE!

NOVEMBER 1

Most of us have been taught that if we are experiencing something tough, then we should focus on getting through it. There is no way to feel the exhilaration of success without overcoming tough. When tough arrives, be grateful, smile and embrace it. You have just been given an opportunity to create a new possibility. If you have the courage to go for it you may fall down... so what? Dust yourself off and go for it again and again until you achieve the success you are focused on. Accept personal responsibility to make it happen NOW!

I AM POSITIVE!

NOVEMBER 2

If your present moment "Doing" and "Being" is the same as your past "Doing" and "Being", then your future "Doing" and "Being" is very predictable. In order to get to your next level you must be willing to change your approach - it is the only way you will create a new possibility to get a different result.

I AM POSITIVE!

NOVEMBER 3

The more you focus on the negative events that have occurred in your life, the more you are preventing yourself from getting on with your life. What happened in your past is not preventing you from future success; the conversation you are having with yourself about it is the reason.

I AM POSITIVE!

NOVEMBER 4

The FIRST step will never be taken if all of the "what ifs" need to be resolved initially. Seeing is not believing... when you believe it first, have faith and demonstrate courage to take the first step, focused on your positive outcomes, your deepest dreams and desires will become reality. This is not a conversation about acquiring or improving a romantic relationship or earning more money - this is about becoming a better you.

I AM POSITIVE!

NOVEMBER 5

Your life is a result of the choices you make.
Increase your awareness by realizing that before
every choice is what I call a "Choice Point". Once you
truly realize this, and accept personal responsibility
for what you choose in that moment – you will feel
the essence of living a life on purpose.

I AM POSITIVE!

NOVEMBER 6

I challenge you to take a powerful step today in the direction of the things you really, really want. In order to get something you have never had, you must be willing to do something you have never done. Until you have the courage to risk success and take that leap, you will never know what incredible gifts are available for you. If you never leave the nest, you will never know what it feels like to fly. You've got this, so go for it. Do you hear that? It is me cheering you on!!

I AM POSITIVE!

NOVEMBER 7

The only reason we get old is because we forget to take the time to play. I understand how busy life can get as we move from one milestone to the next. Graduating from high school, then college. Getting a job, building a career. Getting married, raising children, and then, finally, retirement. Well, I agree, that will keep you very busy; however, remember to have a little fun along the way. Here is a little tip for you, everything goes to another level when you add ENTHUSIASM. I'm just sayin'.

I AM POSITIVE!

NOVEMBER 8

Excellence is a standardized assessment that is a socially agreed upon norm. I challenge you to go beyond excellence today and redefine for yourself and others what it means to deliver excellence in the things you choose to do today. Wouldn't it be really cool if you choose to do that tomorrow too?

I AM POSITIVE!

NOVEMBER 9

Individuals are constantly blaming their reality on circumstances produced by something outside of them. The individuals who ultimately get what they want from life are those who look for the circumstances they want, and, if they can't find them, they create them. There are no victims, only volunteers. Accept personal responsibility to get what you want.

I AM POSITIVE!

NOVEMBER 10

It is important for you to be aware today that the game
is not over if you did not hit the bullseye the first time.
The game is over when you choose not to take another shot.
As you move forward you will encounter challenges and that's
actually very cool. Embrace the challenge and be grateful for it.
If you allow these challenges to be your stopping point, then you
have chosen failure. This is your opportunity to change your
approach, which will change your results. Okay, so pick
yourself up, dust yourself off, and keep moving forward.
Success will not be found in checking out and accepting defeat.
The success you seek is just one more step away, go get it...

I AM POSITIVE!

NOVEMBER 11

"A man who wants to lead the orchestra must turn his back on the crowd." Max Lucado

It is important to become independent of the opinions of others. This is not a conversation about dismissing what others offer you.
This is a conversation about checking their offering against your outcome to determine the value of it.

I AM POSITIVE!

NOVEMBER 12

It is important for us to Dream, however, no mere dream will make tomorrow better. The Dream is necessary, however, insufficient. The Dream is a vital step, however, it is only the first step-in order to make the Dream a reality you must wake up. Next... you must have the courage to TAN (Take Action Now)! and make your dream a reality.

I AM POSITIVE!

NOVEMBER 13

Too many people focus on what they are not and undervalue the positive things they are. How you see yourself dictates the energy and actions you are demonstrating in this present moment. Take a look at that fruit-that is the gift you are giving away.

I AM POSITIVE!

NOVEMBER 14

I don't mind telling you, I love my job. In this present moment is that your truth? If yes, what will you do to get to your next level? If no, what would you be doing if failure was not an option? Life is not a dress rehearsal.

I AM POSITIVE!

NOVEMBER 15

Anger is a secondary emotion, which means there is always a warning sign that it is about to occur. If we choose to continue moving in that space until we become angry it may make us feel better in that moment, however, there is very little long-term benefit derived from that choice. My coaching to you is to not avoid getting angry, however, understand the positive action that you are committed to take that is focused on what you wanted and accept personal responsibility to channel all of that energy to reach that outcome. Oh my, what might that change of approach produce?

I AM POSITIVE!

NOVEMBER 16

A true leader has the confidence to stand alone,
the courage to make tough decisions and the compassion
to listen to the needs of others. They do not set out to be
a leader, yet become one by the quality of their actions
and the integrity of their intent. In the end, leaders are
much like eagles... they don't flock together; you find
them one at a time. There is an "i" in team!

I AM POSITIVE!

NOVEMBER 17

In every one of our futures is a day when we will only have our past to look at. That future and that past are being created in this present moment. If you find yourself focused on the past, it will become your future.
If you choose to focus on creating your future by focusing on what you want and accepting personal responsibility to create it, your future will then authentically become your past.

I AM POSITIVE!

NOVEMBER 18

Here we go again. It's a new day, with New Possibilities for you to focus on everything you want to during the next 24 hours. In this present moment, two choices are available to you: you can choose to believe that it is possible to accomplish those things you want today or you can believe that it is impossible. Whichever you choose to believe, you will create a compelling story to support your belief and 24 hours from now you will get to be "right" again. Congratulations!

I AM POSITIVE!

NOVEMBER 19

The greatest challenges of leadership are: BEing bold, but not a bully; BEing thoughtful, but not lazy; BEing kind, but not weak; BEing proud, but not arrogant; BEing strong, but not rude. Well, ALL of the above is going to be someone's interpretation based on their personal map. Okay, my best coaching is to just "BE".

I AM POSITIVE!

NOVEMBER 20

Life is a series of thousands of circumstances. Every circumstance is an opportunity. No matter what is happening in your life, you can choose to see every circumstance as an opportunity. You can choose to see the positive and know that success is just ahead if you remain FOTO (Focused on the Outcome) and continue to move forward. Have you chosen to see the challenges or the opportunities? What you focus on will expand.

I AM POSITIVE!

NOVEMBER 21

This "Present Moment" creates two very powerful opportunities. The first is to create the future that you want by setting a positive outcome that you are committed to and making appropriate choices that will create that future. The second powerful opportunity, which will be created as a result of taking advantage of the first, is you will create a new past that you will be 100% proud of. Reliving the old past will only create a predictable future that you have already experienced.
It is okay to let it go and move forward.

I AM POSITIVE!

NOVEMBER 22

So many of us spend our energy dreaming of some
magical rose garden over the horizon instead of
creating our own rose garden in this moment.
Happiness does not exist outside of you.
Looking for affirmation and happiness outside
of you will ultimately lead you to disappointment,
frustration, and it will always prove elusive.
Make the choice to BE happy, to BE worthy of
your own rose garden - and then CREATE it!
WAYFO? (What Are You Focused On?)

I AM POSITIVE!

NOVEMBER 23

Negativity is energy that can be directed in any way you choose. Hmmmmm, so rather than spending any more time blaming anyone or anything else for what's creating the negative energy, identify what you want and accept personal responsibility to make it happen. Now use that same energy to make it happen. Oh, was that a smile?

I AM POSITIVE!

NOVEMBER 24

During one of my one on one coaching calls,
my client said something really funny, in fact
I gotta tell you I laugh out loud every time I think
about it. She said, "I plan on taking a more active
role in the decisions I make sometime really soon."
My response to her was, "It would be okay to start
doing that right NOW." Not sure who, however
I intuitively felt that someone else
needed to hear that today.

I AM POSITIVE!

NOVEMBER 25

If your mind is focused on doubt and fear,
you will not focus on the journey to what
you want. The scars of our past indicate where
we have been. Those scars do not have to
determine where we are going.

I AM POSITIVE!

NOVEMBER 26

A happy home does not happen as a result of a building, it is the results of the thoughts of the people living in the building. Communicate what you need from others today with NO attachment to how they respond to your request.

I AM POSITIVE!

NOVEMBER 27

During my initial call on an executive "one to one" coaching call I was asked what I meant when I say, "I am on your team." I responded that what I am saying is "let us go do this" as opposed to "you go do this".

I AM POSITIVE!

NOVEMBER 28

It's party time again! Begin this day with the end in mind. Let's catch a few people doing things right today and celebrate everything that is going right. OMG, this will be an incredible Day!

I AM POSITIVE!

NOVEMBER 29

A healthy attitude is contagious, and you don't wait to catch it from others. Be a carrier. It has been said in many different ways that attitudes are contagious and it is true. Make the choice to infect those around you today with a positive attitude.

I AM POSITIVE!

NOVEMBER 30

There are a lot of us that constantly seek the approval of others. Well the truth is, before you take any action you approve of their approval. Hmmm, so why not just decide what you want and who you want to become, then give yourself approval and make it happen?

I AM POSITIVE!

DECEMBER

DECEMBER 1

Take a moment to compare the difference in the negative energy you feel when you are running from something you do not want, compared to the positive energy you feel when you are running to something you want. Set a positive outcome today and focus on what you what. It feels so good.
My motto is "iFOTO" (I Focus On The Outcome).

I AM POSITIVE!

DECEMBER 2

The greatest challenge to creating your outcomes
and owning your potential in life... is you. Many individuals
are able to see the strengths and find value in the people
around them. Others can't even see the good in others or
themselves. Okay, let's just cut to the chase, today is the
best day in your life to catch a few people doing
things "RIGHT". That would include catching yourself
doing something "RIGHT" also.

I AM POSITIVE!

DECEMBER 3

I have some really great news today,
no matter what has happened up until now, all is
well. You have been prepared to be successful no
matter what happens today. Be grateful for
yesterday because it has been an amazing teacher.
Now get focused on your positive outcome and cash
in on the past. I feel a celebration about to happen.

I AM POSITIVE!

DECEMBER 4

Success, focus, drive, perseverance, and self-worth
(oh my, I could go on) are a matter of the made-up mind.
It does not matter the size or significance of the circumstance
before you. Your ability to succeed and overcome your
circumstances begins first in your decision to do so;
in creating the positive conversation focused on what
you want. You then become a clearing for those things
and people that will help you manifest your success.
Make up your mind and make it happen now.

I AM POSITIVE!

DECEMBER 5

Do something unique today and surprise yourself.
Rather than waiting for "someday" choose it for
yourself today. Wondering what you could do that
would be unique? Well any positive thing, outside
your comfort zone, focused on a win-win will do.
I would love to hear how this turns out.

I AM POSITIVE!

DECEMBER 6

I know that you want more, why not much more?
Stop attempting to predict when and where it will
come from, by doing so you are creating limitations.
Just know that it will come... Our plan of action is
to be in the moment.

I AM POSITIVE!

DECEMBER 7

Great minds have "will do's", while others have "want to's".
One of the factors that make a difference between a
purpose and a wish is personal responsibility.
Wishing for what you want abdicates that
responsibility and leaves it up to someone else
to fulfill your wishes. Take those wishes and accept
personal responsibility for bringing them to life.
Oops, this just got a little scary, didn't it?
Yay Yay, now you are on purpose.

I AM POSITIVE!

DECEMBER 8

I have observed that when an individual hits rock
bottom they feel bad, become emotional and then resign.
I believe that when you hit rock bottom you should
celebrate that whatever you were experiencing is over!
It is time to refocus on an outcome, change your
approach and begin climbing again.
It is not about the destination, it is not about
how fast you get there, it's all about the climb.

I AM POSITIVE!

DECEMBER 9

I know it may be a little early; however, I am really serious about this. Identify something you feel is impossible.
I know, I know, nothing is impossible, right? Well, there are still a few things that you really, really want and you have been apprehensive about going after. Okay, so maybe you don't think it is impossible, however, you are waiting for the right opportunity. Let's declare that today is the right opportunity. You will never know what is beyond your fears unless you break through to the other side.
By the way, impossible is nothing. Now, move your butt.

I AM POSITIVE!

DECEMBER 10

When was the last time somebody made you mad?
Okay, that was a trick question. It has never happened,
you chose it every time. No sense in continuing that
as you realize no one has ever made you happy either.
Yes, if you have ever experienced happiness
it is because you chose it.

I AM POSITIVE!

DECEMBER 11

Today represents the best day to take control of your life and accept 100% personal responsibility to get what you want out of life. Well, that was true yesterday also, so let's get that handled today. Why not you? Why not today?

I AM POSITIVE!

DECEMBER 12

It is not only for what we do that we are held personally responsible, but also for what we do not do. In the context of this conversation there are no victims, only volunteers. One of the greatest gifts you have in every given moment is the gift of choice. And not choosing is choosing. Ultimately you are 100% personally responsible for those choices and what they create for you.
So whatever is happening or not happening, yes, you created that. Okay, take a minute or two to think about this.

I AM POSITIVE!

DECEMBER 13

Being open-minded is neither good nor bad; it just "is".
Be aware of the thought seeds you allow to be planted
in your mind because if they are negative they will produce
negative fruit; if they are positive they will produce positive fruit.
Each thought seed planted will always produce a likeness of itself.

I AM POSITIVE!

DECEMBER 14

There were likely a few commitments you made last year that you did not keep. Every time that happens you lose credibility and trust. A commitment is doing what you said you would do, when you said you would do it, no excuses. Only commit to the things you are truly committed to, because every time we break our commitment, somebody gets hurt.

I AM POSITIVE!

DECEMBER 15

Life is not what you've been taught, it is what you believe; it is not what you've experienced, it is the choices you've made as a result; it is not about what has happened to you, it is how you've remembered it; it is not what challenges have come your way, it is what you've seen as challenging; and it is not about what has appeared on your path, it is what you have accepted. When we accept personal responsibility for our lives, everything is possible.

I AM POSITIVE!

DECEMBER 16

Look around and I know you will agree that change is inevitable, however, growth is optional. Unless you choose to grow, the success you have experienced up until now is dying and decaying. Okay, that is not a pretty picture; time to step up to your next level of growth.

I AM POSITIVE!

DECEMBER 17

Do you really know who you are? Do you really know what you want? Do you really know where you want to go in life? If you answered no like most people, my question to you is if you don't know yourself, why do you expect others to know you at that level? If you answered yes, what are you waiting for to go get those things and to arrive at that place you want to be?

I AM POSITIVE!

DECEMBER 18

I have four new best friends that will make today the absolute best day ever. Now, I am aware that you are acquainted with them, however, up until now you have been avoiding my new best friends. My friends are Challenges, Negative People, Personal Weaknesses, and Procrastination. Every time Challenges, Negative People, Personal Weaknesses and Procrastination show up for you, a new unreasonable possibility is created to build positive capacity to Create a Better Version of Yourself™. The reason these are my new best friends is because they present significant opportunities for me to grow. I am grateful for them. In other words, when they show up, celebrate, then TAN (Take Action Now).to create a positive outcome.

I AM POSITIVE!

DECEMBER 19

There's a difference between being interested and committed. When you are interested in something, you spend time in it when you can, and often with limitations. When you are committed to something, you accept no reasons, alibis, or excuses - only results. If your first roadblock becomes your stop sign, there was no commitment. If you find yourself in a conversation of why you can't or won't make it happen, there was no commitment. Commitment is playing full out and giving heart, body, and soul to make it happen. Whatever it takes means recognizing the roadblock as a gift. Rock on my friend!!

I AM POSITIVE!

DECEMBER 20

Be where you are and be happy in that space;
however, if that happiness is attached to a
person, place or thing, you do not own it.
Happiness is an inside job, so make sure that
what is making you happy is within your control.

I AM POSITIVE!

DECEMBER 21

If the source of your happiness is based on
circumstances or the opinions of others,
then you really are not happy. Happiness is a
gift available to everyone at ALL times, no matter
the circumstances or someone else's opinion.
Choose today to be happy. It is your gift to yourself,
your family, friends, and then to the world
around you. You Matter!

I AM POSITIVE!

DECEMBER 22

If you are holding resentment toward anyone or anything, you are bound to that person or circumstance by an emotional link that is stronger than steel. Choose to forgive and get on with living. The investment you are making in resentment will never produce a positive return.

I AM POSITIVE!

DECEMBER 23

To achieve the seemingly impossible is precisely the unrealistic thing that you must think about. Being unrealistically successful begins first in the conversation you are having with yourself. Envision it, create a positive conversation around it, and celebrate it. Giving life to the thing you want opens the door to manifesting it and makes the impossible, possible. One of the greatest secrets revealed is that the only impossibilities that exist in the universe exist in the conversation you are having with yourself.

I AM POSITIVE!

DECEMBER 24

Have you noticed how even the simplest acts of kindness put a warm feeling in your heart? Me too. Turn up the heat in your heart today because Givers Gain, catch someone doing something right today!

I AM POSITIVE!

DECEMBER 25

During this holiday season, many people are focused on what they can provide for their children, family, and friends. I encourage you, on this Christmas Day, to focus on giving something more meaningful than ever before, give the gift of your undivided attention and make positive memories.

I AM POSITIVE!

DECEMBER 26

Theodore Roosevelt said in his Fireside Motto
"It is not the critic who counts, it's not the man who points
out how the strong man stumbled or where the doer of
deeds could have done them better – the credit belongs to
the person who is actually in the arena." Play full out and live
your life on purpose and stay focused on your positive
outcomes in spite of your critics. Oh, and by the way, those
critics are some of the best gifts you will ever receive,
I'm just sayin'.

I AM POSITIVE!

DECEMBER 27

I heard it said many times during my childhood that money is the root of ALL evil. Well, I have come to realize that is not the truth. What I have learned is money is not the root of ANY evil; the choices we make are the root of all of our outcomes, good or bad. This could be tough; however, I am requesting you repeat after me..."I am Personally Responsible". Oh my, did you feel that? It was a shift in the universe.

I AM POSITIVE!

DECEMBER 28

You will always be able to rise above a negative image that others have of you. However, you will never rise above the negative image you have of yourself. It is important to be aware that the image you have of yourself, is being projected by the conversation you are having with yourself. When you change that conversation, you will change how you see yourself. So, check the conversation. You are worth it. Okay, so here is one of my favorite affirmations and you can use it shamelessly, "I will not be defined by my yesterdays. Today, I begin again."

I AM POSITIVE!

DECEMBER 29

There is a lot of talk these days about happiness.
Let's get this handled once and for all. Choose to be
happy right now. Okay, do it again. Okay, keep doing that.
Now I can hear someone saying, "Mike that is not
realistic" and they are right. I can hear others saying,
"Mike I did it and it's working" and they are right, too. Nuff said.

I AM POSITIVE!

DECEMBER 30

If you do not take a firm, significant, positive stand for something, you just might fall for anything. A true leader has the confidence to take a positive stand for something, even if it means standing alone. So who are you and what do you stand for? It is important to know because who you "BE" they will "BE"come. You are a role model.

I AM POSITIVE!

DECEMBER 31

It's "Not Over". There are NO problems,
just opportunities. Today I begin again.

I AM POSITIVE!

CPSIA information can be obtained
at www.ICGtesting.com
Printed in the USA
BVHW010438281018
531393BV00001B/1/P

9 780983 330516